In Season

and Out

T0338844

In Season and Out

SERMONS FOR THE CHRISTIAN YEAR

DAVID A. deSILVA

LEXHAM PRESS

LEXHAM PRESS

In Season and Out: Sermons for the Christian Year

Copyright 2019 David A. deSilva

Lexham Press, 1313 Commercial St., Bellingham, WA 98225
LexhamPress.com

Print ISBN 9781683592914
Digital ISBN 9781683592921

Lexham Editorial Team: Elliot Ritzema, Abigail Stocker, Danielle Thevenaz
Cover Design: Kristen Cork
Typesetting: Scribe Inc.

To the Rev. Jeffrey M. Halenza,
a most gifted preacher and dear colleague in ministry

Contents

Preface

Sermons arise within particular contexts and are composed to speak to those contexts. Just as the Scriptures—which themselves arose within and were written to give guidance and direction to people in particular contexts—can continue to speak to people beyond those original times and places, so it may be hoped that sermons grounded in those Scriptures can speak to people beyond the occasion for which they were originally composed. But also like the Scriptures, it is important to know something about the contexts in which the sermons arose.

I had the privilege to serve as interim pastor at Port Charlotte United Methodist Church in Port Charlotte, Florida, from October 2017 through June 2018, and these sermons largely derive from that period. It is a church accustomed to observing the liturgical seasons of the year (Advent, Christmas, Epiphany, etc.) and to liturgical worship, chiefly as found in *The United Methodist Hymnal* and *The United Methodist Book of Worship* but with many clear and obvious connections to the liturgies of the Anglican tradition and beyond. While I am extensively familiar with the Revised Common Lectionary, I look to it more for suggestions and ideas than rules. As a result, a number of these sermons are based cleanly on the lectionary texts for a given Sunday; others may join two lectionary texts from different Sundays in order to better facilitate (in my opinion) the development of a particular topic; and still others show a looser connection with lectionary texts but may still be of value to preachers who follow the lectionary more closely than I did. I have included a table of these correspondences as an appendix to facilitate the use of this collection by lectionary preachers.

Some years ago, the church adopted as its mission statement, "Know Christ; grow more like Christ; go to serve Christ." There are frequent echoes of the church's mission statement in the sermons that follow, and the final three sermons in this collection take the three elements of that mission statement one by one. While I have edited the sermons to remove references to particular individuals in the congregation (they were always praiseworthy references, not calling people out!) and other indications of context that might be unduly distancing for the reader, I have not tried to disguise the fact that these are, in fact, *sermons* that were composed for oral delivery to a gathered congregation in the context of our services of worship. Scripture translations throughout are my own unless otherwise noted.

I have had the privilege of serving as music director under several pastors who were gifted preachers and liturgists, but the style and voice of one in particular has always stood out in my memory as a model to emulate—the Rev. Jeffrey M. Halenza, pastor of Christ Our Hope Lutheran Church since its founding in 1976, with whom I worked from 1990–1995. It is to him, in honor of his ministry and with deep appreciation for his pastoral character and gifts, that I dedicate this collection.

Sermons for Liturgical Seasons

PART ONE

Sermons for
Liturgical Seasons

1

"Our Wake-Up Call" (Advent)

Isaiah 64:1–9; Mark 13:24–37

*T*oday marks the beginning of another season of Advent, that period of watchfulness, of renewed waiting, that begins the church year. This Sunday's readings remind us that the season of Advent is not just about, nor even *chiefly* about, getting ready for Christmas. Indeed, I've long felt that it was rather artificial, Advent after Advent, to act as if we were looking "forward" to Christ's first coming in humility as a baby born in Bethlehem. Putting ourselves in the position of those who, more than two thousand years ago, were anticipating the coming of a Messiah and acting as if we were yearning for the baby yet to be born has long seemed to me to be a kind of playacting, of holy make-believe.

The readings appointed for *this* Sunday, starting off *this* Advent, *do* remind us of that for which we are indeed still waiting, that for which we need very much to get ready—Christ's coming again in glory.

> O that you would tear open the heavens and come
>   down,

> so that the mountains would quake at your pres-
>   ence. (Isa 64:1 NRSV)

> Then they will see "the Son of Man coming in clouds"
> with great power and glory. (Mark 13:26 NRSV)

> What I say to you, I say to all: Keep watching! (Mark 13:37)

If we find that Christmas is upon us this year and we're not altogether ready for it, it won't be the end of the world. But if Christ's coming again finds us unprepared, living as people who haven't been looking for it—well, that's another story, isn't it? Advent is our wake-up call to what is coming, to who is coming, rousing us to shake off our sleep and restore our souls to vigilance. And we cannot afford to keep hitting the snooze button on *this* alarm.

Preparations for Christmas tend to overwhelm Advent, to bury beneath an avalanche of gift buying, travel planning, cantata preparing, menu mapping, and home decorating what Advent, as a gift of the liturgical year, seeks to give us—a chance to examine ourselves and to realign our lives, both as individual disciples and as a church family, so that we will move *this* year toward greater readiness to meet our Lord at his coming in glory to judge the living and the dead. So let's pause together and unwrap these two texts, and see if, perhaps, they might help us to receive this gift of Advent and make the best use possible of it, rather than setting it aside in favor of our Christmas preparations.

*   *   *

The passage from Isaiah 64 really begins in the previous chapter. The prophet tells once again the familiar story of Israel. God showed them great favor, leading them out of Egypt and into the land of promise. Rather than keep faith with God by living as he commanded in his covenant, they rebelled against God and God's law, so that God brought upon them the punishments that God had promised—destruction and exile. And now things are simply not the way they were meant to be. God's chosen people are *not* walking in God's ways and relishing God's presence; Israel is not experiencing the promises that had been extended to it. It's all just wrong. "How can God stand it?" Isaiah asks. How can he *not* "tear open the heavens and come down" and set everything right, the way it ought to be?

We might ask the same questions—perhaps not on our own behalf (though we have no doubt had our moments) but on behalf of the many who have suffered *significantly* due to the evil or callousness of others. And we can be sure that the blood of the innocent cries out with these words before the throne of God day and night—"O that you would tear open the heavens and come down!"—the blood of a young family killed during a house robbery; the blood of countless children dead or maimed by the violence of mercenaries in Africa or land mines in abandoned war zones; the blood of a young woman raped and killed; the blood of generations who died as slaves; the blood of thousands who disappeared as a totalitarian regime protected its interests against potential dissenters; the blood of those who died simply because others refused to share with them the gifts that God intended for all. Iraqi Christians, refugees from the Islamic State, are crying out this prayer today; a Nigerian Christian woman and her children, whose husband and father was lynched in the street, are crying out this prayer today; Christians in the wake of mass shootings in our own country are crying out this prayer today. How can it be that Christ will *not* come, that a God whose heart is justice itself should *not* bring all to account before him?

It's been almost two millennia since Jesus uttered the words we heard read from Mark's Gospel today, and he *still* hasn't come back. This raises some difficult but legitimate questions. First, if God is going to tear open the heavens, if the Son of Man is going to descend upon the clouds surrounded by the hosts of heaven, why hasn't he? Second, if he hasn't in the last two thousand or so years, why should we be concerned—this year or next or the year after that—that he *will*? How important a compass point can his coming again be for us? Of all the things for which we might spend our lives getting ready, why should we say that this one is still so important that it should be placed at the top of our list of priority events for which to be prepared?

We all need to solve these questions for ourselves. My own solution to the second question is not theologically profound, but one of simple math. I figure that, at the absolute maximum, I have forty or so years of life left (and that's, in all probability, highballing the figure). If Jesus hasn't returned within that time frame, I shall certainly go to him before the end of it. And the next thing I expect to see after death closes my eyes is the scene portrayed for us at the beginning of today's reading from Mark 13:

> The sun will be darkened, and the moon will not give its light, and the stars will be falling from heaven, and the powers in the heavens will be shaken. Then they will see "the Son of Man coming in clouds" with great power and glory. Then he will send out the angels, and gather his elect from the four winds, from the ends of the earth to the ends of heaven. (Mark 13:24–27 NRSV)

It won't much matter to me how much time elapses between death closing my eyes and the last trumpet opening them again. Jesus' coming again is, for me, at *most* the rest of my lifetime away.

As for the first question, it seems to me that God will only tear open the heavens and come down when one of a few possible conditions has been reached. One condition would be that God has seen positively accomplished on this earth and in the human story all that he wants to see accomplished, such that there is no longer any good left to come from delaying. Another condition would be that God has given up hope on humanity in general and sees that his church has exhausted its ability or its willingness to mediate his deliverance further to the people of this world, such that there is no longer any good left to come from delaying. The day on which God chooses to "tear open the heavens and come down," when the Son of Man will be seen "coming in clouds," will indeed at last mean justice for every soul, bringing to each either vindication or condemnation. But every day on which God does *not* tear open the heavens means opportunity for every soul.

I'm not speaking here just of an opportunity to "get saved" or "accept Jesus" or any such pale shadow of what God seeks from each one of us. I mean here an opportunity to do the work that our Lord has entrusted to us—to each one of us as a disciple, to all of us as a congregation, and to all congregations together as the global body of Christ.

> Beware, keep alert; for you do not know when the time will come. It is like a man going on a journey, when he leaves home and puts his slaves in charge, each with his work, and commands the doorkeeper to be on the watch. Therefore, keep awake—for you do not know when the master of the house will come, in the evening, or at midnight, or at cockcrow, or at dawn, or else he may find you asleep when he comes suddenly. And what I say to you I say to all: Keep awake. (Mark 13:32–37 NRSV)

This last sentence is one point in Mark's Gospel where we find Jesus himself thinking beyond his immediate circle of hearers—namely, his disciples who have gathered around him on the Mount of Olives for this teaching—and thinking about the many who will hear him through them. We can almost see and hear Jesus at this point speaking to us, looking past his disciples and directly into the camera, as it were, to deliver this admonition to us: "Keep awake!"

The question for us in this interim is not, "How long will it be?" or, heaven forbid, "Can we figure out exactly when it will be?" It is also not, "Why isn't God doing anything to help? To make things better? To make it easier for us to believe and to invest ourselves in his work?" The question for us is: Are we doing the work that Jesus has entrusted to us, like servants who hope to be found faithfully and diligently doing that work when he returns? Or are we doing our *own* work, attending to our *own* agendas, seeking our *own* interests, making up our *own* list of things to do each day that have little or nothing to do with the work that God has laid upon us to do? Servants cannot afford to act that way; servants must attend first and foremost to the work the master has given them and then to their *own* interests only as time permits—*not* the reverse.

When Christ comes, he will encounter each one of us as either part of the problem or part of the solution in regard to the ills that beset this world. There will be no middle ground—and those who stand on the sidelines watching the ills that beset the world, shaking their heads and complaining that God isn't doing anything about it, are part of the problem, not part of the solution.

What, then, is the work that the master has laid upon us, to occupy us in this interim? God wants for us to know him, to live fully in relationship with him and in response to him. God wants for us to grow into the people that he is re-creating us to be through the working of the Holy Spirit in our midst—to be changed from self-centered and self-driven people into other-centered and Spirit-driven people whose joy it is to do what pleases God. God wants for us to go out to bear witness to and extend his kingdom, his hope, his love, his provision, his justice everywhere that there is need. We can say so much about the work generally; each one of us has to discern our particular tasks toward attaining these ends. Scripture is an indispensable and inexhaustible resource for us in this process of discernment. Every page reveals something about the character, the heart, the driving passions of the God we serve. Every page reveals something to us about the character, heart, and driving passions of the people that Jesus died to empower us to become. Every page has something to say about how to invest ourselves in real-world actions that will advance what God wants to accomplish through us.

* * *

Jesus' word to us this Advent, Jesus' word to us *today*, is that those who wake up to understand and pursue these things, who refuse to be as one asleep to God or to God's purposes for us any longer, are indeed favored. He invites us to renewed attentiveness—to watchfulness—in regard to this work of knowing, growing, and going as he desires and directs us day by day. He invites us to put at the top of our list of things to do *his* list of things to do. The question that his coming again will pose to each one of us when we lay eyes upon him is this: "Did your life show my death to be worthwhile? Did you devote your individual lives and your common life together to *everything* that my death opened up for you, and did you diligently discharge the responsibility that my death placed upon you—to live no longer for yourself, but for the One who died and was raised on your behalf?" (see 2 Cor 5:15).

The first gift of Christmas is this gift of Advent—the gift of an opportunity to ask ourselves these questions and work to realign ourselves such that we will be better able to answer "yes" in the coming year than we were in the year that is now past. And when we can answer "yes," then we will be living as people who are fully awake rather than still asleep to what's really important in this world, for this life.

During Advent, we often sing the familiar hymn, "O Come, O Come, Emmanuel." I would invite you not to sing it as we might imagine the people of ancient Judea singing out their prayers for a Messiah who would come to deliver them, nor as if the object of this hymn—this prayer—was fulfilled in the birth of Jesus so long ago. I would invite you, instead, to sing it to the Christ who sits enthroned at God's right hand, whose coming *again* in glory we confess as a pillar of our faith, and whose future interventions we count on for the fulfillment of our hope. I would invite you to sing it as people who are newly committed to live and invest yourselves such that you will have no cause for shame, and he no cause for disappointment, when he does come in fulfillment of his word.

2

"A Messiah Nobody Expected" (Advent)

Luke 1:68–79; Isaiah 11:1–5, 10–12

Our New Testament reading today is known as the "song of Zechariah." Luke introduces this as a prophetic word spoken by Zechariah, uttered as he was moved by the Holy Spirit. It is a deeply poetic expression of hope for what was happening in Israel as a result of God's activity in Zechariah's own family. Zechariah, as you may recall, was a priest in Judea, and his wife Elizabeth was also born into a priestly family. They were getting on in years, and Elizabeth had not been able to have any children—not until, that is, the angel Gabriel appeared to Zechariah while Zechariah was burning incense in the temple. Gabriel told him that his wife Elizabeth was going to conceive. In nine months, she would bear a son, whom they would name "John," which in Hebrew means "God has shown favor." Zechariah said, essentially, "Yeah, right. Why should I believe that?" Gabriel replied, "I'll tell you what; I'll give you a sign. You will be mute, unable to speak another word for nine months until what I have foretold comes about." This, in turn, prompted the "song of Elizabeth," an exuberant hymn of praise to God that has not been recorded in Scripture.

Zechariah now knows that his own son is going to be special, having been announced by an angel as very few babies had been announced in Israel's history. Six months later, cousin Mary comes to visit the pregnant Elizabeth with surprising news of her own—she, too, is to bear a son, about whom the same angel, Gabriel, said even more amazing things:

> He will be great and will be called the son of the Most High, and the Lord God will give him the throne of his ancestor David, and he will rule over the house of Jacob forever— there will not be an end to his kingdom! (Luke 1:32–33)

*   *   *

Zechariah has three more months to ponder these things until Elizabeth comes to full term and gives birth to their son. At the baby's circumcision, with all the family gathered around, Elizabeth announces that the child will be named "John," as the angel had instructed. The extended family has trouble with this, since it's not a name in the family, so they go to Zechariah and make signs to him to find out what *he* wants to name the baby. He reaches for his writing tablet and writes down, "His name is John." Actually, the first thing he probably wrote down was, "Really? Sign language? I'm mute, not deaf, you idiots!" Nevertheless, when he fulfills the angel's word by naming his son "John," he is able once again to speak, at which point he shouts in a raspy voice his celebrated hymn of praise:

> May the Lord God of Israel be well spoken of,
>> because he took an interest in, and worked redemption for, his people.
> He raised up a horn of deliverance for us in the house
>> of David, his servant,

just as he spoke through the mouth of his holy
    prophets from of old—
deliverance from our enemies and from the hand of all
    who persist in hating us,
    to show mercy toward our forebears and to remem-
        ber his holy covenant,
the oath that he swore to our father Abraham,
    that he would grant us, once rescued from the hand
        of our enemies,
to serve him fearlessly all our days, doing what is holy
    and righteous before him.

And you, child, will be called a prophet of the Most
    High,
    for you will go ahead of the Lord to prepare his
        paths,
to give knowledge of deliverance to his people
    in the forgiveness of their sins through the deeply
        felt compassion of our God,
by which the Dayspring from on high has taken an
        interest in us
    so as to shine light upon those sitting in darkness
        and in death's shadow,
to guide our feet into the path of peace. (Luke 1:68–79)

In this song, Zechariah says that God is doing great things for Israel, raising up a "horn of deliverance" for God's people. This is an image that has long since ceased to communicate, but in the literature of ancient Israel a "horn" was a symbol of strength and ascendancy. In a number of texts, it is specifically connected with the Davidic king and with God's restoration of David's line of kings:

The LORD will judge the ends of the earth;
    he will give strength to his king
    and exalt the horn of his anointed. (1 Sam 2:10 ESV)

There I will make a horn to sprout for David;
    I have prepared a lamp for my anointed.
       (Ps 132:17 ESV)

This seems to be Zechariah's expectation as well:

He raised up a horn of deliverance for us in the house
      of David, his servant,
    just as he spoke through the mouth of his holy
      prophets from of old. (Luke 1:69-70)

*   *   *

But what was Zechariah really expecting? What was Zechariah looking for in a Messiah, God's Anointed One? I dare say that he had *no* expectation of seeing Mary's child nailed up and dying on a Roman cross; he had *no* expectation that his own son, as the forerunner and herald of this Messiah, would end up imprisoned and beheaded by a king *not* from David's line—Herod Antipas, a Jewish puppet king propped up by Rome whom Jesus would leave on the throne of Galilee alongside the Roman governor ruling Judea.

We have the benefit of looking back on Jesus and his messiahship from a vantage point almost two thousand years after his resurrection from the dead. We have the benefit of centuries and centuries of rereading the Old Testament and seeing from beginning to end what we *now* think of as "prophecies" about Jesus, about the kind of deliverance that Jesus accomplished for humanity, and about the shape that his messiahship would take—a process that, according to Luke, started with Jesus himself as he walked with two of his clueless disciples on the road to Emmaus after his resurrection:

> "Oh, how foolish you are, and how slow of heart to believe all that the prophets have declared! Was it not necessary that the Messiah should suffer these things and then enter into his glory?" Then beginning with Moses and all the prophets, he interpreted to them the things about himself in all the scriptures. (Luke 24:25-27 NRSV)

I have frequently heard people remark, "How could the Jewish people *not* recognize their Messiah when Jesus lined up with so many prophecies in their own Scriptures?" What is clear in hindsight—and from the position of having experienced being accepted and adopted by God in Jesus, of having experienced the resurrected Lord and being enlightened by the Holy Spirit—was so far from clear for those in Zechariah's day looking *ahead* to God's deliverance that no single Jewish author prior to Jesus' death and resurrection, and no single Jewish author outside of the Jesus movement that formed after Jesus' death and resurrection, gave expression to this kind of Messiah.

He was truly a Messiah that no one expected, at least, no one that's left us anything in writing from the period—and that's a *lot* of writing. If we were to read through all surviving Jewish literature between the Old Testament and the second century AD— the Apocrypha, the collection known by the uninviting title "Pseudepigrapha," the Dead Sea Scrolls, the writings of Philo and Josephus, and the earliest rabbinic texts—we would find not one, I repeat, not *one* Jewish author writing about a Messiah who would teach, heal, lead a peaceful resistance movement, die a condemned criminal, rise from the dead, and ascend to God's right hand until some future coming in judgment.

Now, the Jewish people were not all expecting the *same* kind of Messiah. Hopes for what the Messiah would do and who the Messiah would be depended in large measure on what a particular group of Jews thought was most wrong in the world as they were experiencing it. There was a great deal of consensus about a few things that were wrong, however. Gentiles, whom God had *not* chosen, were in charge of the land and the people that God *had* chosen. As a result of centuries of gentile conquest and domination, the majority of the people that God had chosen were scattered across the Mediterranean and Middle East outside of the land that God had given to them. The Jewish rulers who had enjoyed authority prior to Rome's intervention and the Jewish rulers who now enjoyed authority in cooperation with Rome were not the people to whom God had promised such authority, which belonged to the family of David.

This rather broadly shared sense of what was wrong in the world, given God's historic promises to the people of Israel, gave rise to a broadly shared set of convictions about what God's Messiah would do when God chose to send deliverance to God's people. We can listen to one Jew from about fifty years before Jesus' birth give expression to these expectations for a Messiah:

> Look, O Lord, and raise up for them their king, the son of David ... that he may reign over Israel your servant. Endow him with strength, that he may shatter unrighteous rulers and that he may purge Jerusalem of the gentile nations that trample her down to destruction. In the wisdom of righteousness he will thrust out sinners from the inheritance. ... He will destroy the godless nations with the word of his mouth. ... And he will gather together a holy people, whom he will lead in righteousness. ... And he will divide them according to their tribes upon the

land. And neither sojourner nor alien will live among them anymore. ... And he will have the people of the gentiles to serve him under his yoke. ... Blessed are they that will be in those days, in that they will see the good fortune of Israel, in the gathering together of the tribes, which God will accomplish. (Psalms of Solomon 17, selections)

According to this profile, our hymn "Come, Thou Long-Expected Jesus," is inaccurate. A Messiah may have been "long expected," but not the Messiah that *Jesus* turned out to be. Where did the Jews get their expectations? If we were to be completely honest, we would have to admit that they do have deep scriptural roots. We have to be very selective when reading Old Testament prophecies in Advent. Consider the lesson from Isaiah: "A shoot shall come out from the stump of Jesse [David's father], and a branch shall grow out of his roots," a promised ruler upon whom God's Spirit will rest, who will judge in righteousness, who will bring peace to the land. But what *doesn't* the lectionary include from Isaiah 11? "They shall swoop down on the backs of the Philistines in the west, together they shall plunder the people of the east. They shall put forth their hand against Edom and Moab, and the Ammonites will serve them" (Isa 11:14): a vision of a restored kingdom of Israel—specifically, violently subjugating the non-Jewish nations all around Israel's territory.

Zechariah likely expected John, who would become known as John "the Baptizer," to be the forerunner and herald of such a nationalistic Messiah: a Messiah who would restore the monarchy and kingdom of the house of David; a Messiah through whom God's promises to Abraham and Abraham's legitimate offspring, the people of Israel, would be reaffirmed—a numerous people enjoying self-governance in their own land; a Messiah who would gather the dispersed Jews throughout the world back to their ancestral land, which would be redistributed to the twelve tribes just as it had been in the days of Joshua, Jesus' namesake. Jesus' own disciples did not want to give up this same set of expectations. Recall how, after Jesus forewarned his disciples about what would happen to him in Jerusalem, Peter took Jesus aside to give him a lesson in true messiahship (Mark 8:31–33): "No, Lord; that's *not* what's going to happen here!" Recall how, after Jesus forewarned his disciples the *third time* about his death at gentile hands, James and John came to him, jockeying to become his wingmen when Jesus took over Israel (Mark 10:35–40). Recall how, after the crucifixion, those two disciples on the road to Emmaus expressed their disappointment in Jesus: "We had hoped that he was the one who would redeem Israel" (Luke 24:21). Recall how, even *after* Jesus' resurrection, his disciples still asked: "So will you *now* restore political independence to Israel?" (Acts 1:6). It wasn't until after Jesus was gone again that *his own disciples* began to realize that the Messiah God had sent was not the Messiah they had expected.

If we think about where Jesus' messiahship took the "Jesus people," we might get a sense of all the hopes and expectations that Jesus' Jewish followers had to give up in order to say "Yes" to him. He took them away from the hope for a renewed Jewish monarchy in Israel, away from the hope for the subjugation of the gentile nations, away from the hope that God's future meant a return to the "good old days" after Israel's conquest of Canaan and division of the spoils of the land among them. Jesus inaugurated a kingdom of a very different kind, one that did not privilege one ethnic group to the exclusion of others, one that was not built on political power and military might, one that broke down the dividing walls between people rather than reinforcing them (see Eph 2:11–22). His messiahship answered the universal problem of what had gone wrong for all humanity, not merely the problems of local and ethnic interest to Israel.

*   *   *

All of this raises the question: Do *we* understand what kind of Messiah has come in Jesus, or do we impose upon him expectations and hopes that are foreign to *his* mission as God's anointed? Have we spent enough time with him, have we meditated long and hard enough on his word, that we also have discarded our false expectations for him and yielded to the kind of Messiah that he *really* is and, therefore, what it means to experience his deliverance—his salvation—and follow him as God's Anointed One?

Do we expect a Messiah who will put his power behind our nation and its interests, who will adopt our nation's agenda in this world as his own? Jesus didn't advance his *own* nation's interests in the world!

Do we expect a Messiah who will save us from life's pains and unpleasantries, make everything work out comfortably for us, make things go our way, or keep us flush with funds? Jesus told anyone who wanted to follow him that it would mean denying themselves, taking up the cross that he bore, serving as he came to serve, and enduring any hardship or embarrassment that came their way for his sake.

Do we expect a Messiah who will give us the unfathomable riches of his spiritual blessings while we give to him the leftovers, the most token offerings, of our time, energies, and resources? Jesus called his disciples to a radical reinvestment of themselves—to leave everything else behind, then and there, and to follow him, giving all their time, energy, and resources to advancing God's kingdom thenceforth.

Do we expect a Messiah who will be our personal Savior without also being our Lord? Jesus asked his disciples: "What's the value of calling me 'Lord, Lord' if you're not going to do what I tell you?" (Luke 6:36).

In all probability, Zechariah died long before he ever came to understand the messiahship of the One whom his son John would announce to the people and thus long before his life could be transformed by the encounter with, and by the tutelage of, such a Messiah. I pray that the same will *not* be true for any one of us.

3

"A Mother for God's Son" (Advent)

Luke 1:26–38

*I*t is said of Jewish mothers that they typically think of their sons as God's gift to the world. Mary was one Jewish mother who could legitimately make this claim. It has been my experience that Protestants don't give much attention to Mary apart from the season of Christmas with our nativity scenes that minimally include Joseph, Mary, and the Christ child (ox and ass sold separately). I think that we Protestants largely avoid Mary because a lot of us are squeamish about the level of attention that our Catholic sisters and brothers give her.

Mary, of course, is a figure of central importance in Catholic theology, liturgy, and spirituality. She is often depicted in Catholic art enthroned in heaven alongside Christ; she is routinely asked by worshipers to intercede with God the Father and with her son Jesus on the basis of the position she is believed to occupy as "queen of Heaven" and on the basis of the relationship that she still enjoys with the glorified Christ as his *mother*. Based on the almost universally shared Christian conviction that Jesus was God the Son in human flesh, our Catholic and Eastern Orthodox brothers and sisters will speak of Mary as the "Mother of God," which, while we Protestants would have to concede that this is technically true, nevertheless makes us profoundly uncomfortable.

In reaction against all of this, we tend to ignore or diminish Mary, probably erring too far in the opposite direction. I have heard Protestants object: "Mary was a sinner like us whom Jesus would have to redeem, an ordinary woman like any other." While I regard the first statement to be true, I think that the second is *not*. Mary was an extraordinary woman who, in yielding herself in obedience to God's will and in embracing her Son's mission, shows us a great deal about the heart of the genuine disciple. She also had to become an extraordinary mother to love, nurture, and support such an extraordinary Son on such an extraordinary mission—one that would cost her most of the natural joys that mothers might expect of their children.

* * *

This Scripture recalls for us the familiar story of the annunciation, the angel Gabriel's appearing to Mary to tell her what God would accomplish through her in the Son that she would uniquely engender and bear. While we think of the virgin birth in terms of the miraculous and wonderful significance of Jesus as Son of God, we should never lose sight of the cost that accompanied Mary's embracing her role. When Elizabeth, Zechariah's barren and aging wife, became pregnant, she declared that God had taken *away* her reproach among her neighbors (Luke 1:25); when Mary became pregnant, it could only have *brought* her reproach.

We might not appreciate the importance of Mary's assertion, "I do not 'know' a man" (Luke 1:34). Sexual purity was the indispensable element of a woman's virtue and honor in Mary's world. One example will have to suffice. A century or so before

Jesus, an anonymous Jew wrote a historical romance about a woman named Judith, who became the savior of her city and ultimately of the Jewish people by seducing an enemy general into a drunken stupor and cutting off his head. Her first words when back in the city with the general's head in her knapsack? "I only seduced him with my *looks*. He committed no sin with me, to defile and shame me" (Jdt 13:16). Having delivered her city from a desperate siege, Judith still couldn't let anyone think that she had extramarital sex to accomplish it.

Mary was about to sacrifice her reputation for the sake of serving God's design for deliverance. The Gospel according to Matthew gives more attention to the unwelcome consequences of the angel's good news for Mary. While Joseph, her betrothed, might have planned to break off the engagement as quietly as possible so as to spare Mary any *unnecessary* shame, coming to full term as a single mother would have nevertheless brought a great deal of *unavoidable* shame in first-century Judea or Galilee. One wonders about the extent to which first Mary, then Jesus, had to endure taunts regarding his irregular birth. Mark remembers the villagers of Nazareth asking one another in response to Jesus' sermon there, "Is not this the carpenter, the son of Mary?" (Mark 6:3). Matthew would render this differently—"Is not this the *carpenter's son*? Is not his mother called Mary?" (Matt 13:55)— but Mark may preserve something closer to the real thing. To be called "the son of Mary" is quite a significant thing in a village where every male takes his father's name as an identifier (think of "Simon Bar-Jonah"—Simon, son of John—or "Jesus Bar-Abbas"—Jesus, son of Abbas). One wonders if John's Gospel doesn't preserve some reflection of this as well when those with whom Jesus finds himself in an argument about whether or not they are truly Abraham's children say: "*We* weren't born from fornication" (John 7:41).

Mary valued God's promise enough—what this child would become and what this child would accomplish for God's purposes in the world—to endure the shame that was likely to come. This cannot help but foreshadow for us the very posture later taken by her Son—who, "for the sake of the joy set before him, endured a cross, despising shame" (Heb 12:2). It would be a posture that many in the early church would have to imitate in order to follow Jesus, that many over the centuries—most numerously in the twentieth and twenty-first!—have had to imitate. But Mary was willing to bear reproach for the Christ before the Christ was even born (compare Heb 11:26; 13:13).

Eight days after Jesus' birth, an old man named Simeon hinted to Mary that she might not be raising this child with a view to enjoying the typical lifelong relationship that mothers cherish having with their children. After he celebrates having lived long enough to see the one through whom God's redemption would come into the world—the one who would be "a light for revelation to the nations and the glory of God's people Israel" (Luke 2:32)—Simeon looks at Mary and adds: "This one is set for the fall and rise of many in Israel and for a sign that will provoke controversy in order that the inner thoughts of many hearts may be uncovered—and a sword shall pierce your own soul as well!" (Luke 2:34–35). *Thank you, scary old man loitering in the temple. May I have my child back now, please?*

Much of what Simeon had said about Jesus might have been unsurprising to Mary after what the archangel Gabriel had announced prior to Jesus' conception and after what the shepherds had reported seeing and hearing at his birth. But this last bit was new: this good news, this divine revolution, wasn't going to be painless for Mary or her son. Accepting *his* destiny meant steeling herself for suffering as well—another foreshadowing for us of what it means for most of the world's Christians to follow, to hold on to, this Jesus.

The very next episode in Luke fast-forwards twelve years to the story of Jesus in the temple. (Parenting pro tip: don't leave a major city during its most crowded tourist season assuming that your preteen is somewhere in the caravan.) We can surely sympathize with Mary once she and Joseph have found Jesus: "Child, why did you put us through this? Your father and I have gone crazy looking for you!" (Luke 2:48). Jesus' answer—"Why did you have to look for me? Weren't you aware that I'd have to be attending to my Father's business?" (Luke 2:49)—was a reminder that her Son had a calling in response to his heavenly Father that would take him away from his family and that his mission eclipsed his attachment to them. The most surprising thing here for me—who, as a child, could get lost and, as a parent, could look for a lost son—is how unperturbed Jesus is after having been left essentially on his own in a big city for three days! How that strange calm must have unsettled Mary, who had been frantically searching for a boy who was completely untroubled that he was without her for such a long time. Did it remind her once again: "My son was not born *for me*"? Did it remind her that the love and nurture she was pouring into him—and would continue to pour into him—was for the sake of his accomplishing his "Father's business," the destiny that she embraced for him as well?

Nowadays when a son or daughter only leaves home at thirty, we consider it a "failure to launch." Not so in first-century Galilee. As the eldest son—and, in all likelihood, after Joseph's death, since Joseph has completely disappeared from the scene—Jesus would have been the pillar of the family business and the acting head of the household. All things being equal, he would have become and remained the gravitational center of the Bar-Joseph family for his and the next generation—and, quite importantly, the staff of Mary's old age. But Mary had to give up her dreams for a normal, secure life with her firstborn son at the center of a normal household for the sake of Jesus' mission to secure God's good for many households.

It was Mary who, according to John's Gospel, prompted Jesus' first miracle. Mary and Jesus went as guests to a wedding in the village of Cana in Galilee, with Jesus' first disciples tagging along. These wedding banquets were multiple-day affairs, and, at some point, the wine ran out. Mary came to Jesus and said, "They have no wine." Jesus' reply was essentially, "How is that *our* problem?" He understood what was implicit in his mother's bringing the problem to his attention—Mary's conviction that her son could do something about it on the spot. He added, "It's not my time yet," as if he understood that she was saying to him, "This is as good a time as any, Jesus, to start doing what you were born to do." Jewish mothers apparently don't hear their sons when they say "no," so Mary says to the servants standing nearby, "Do whatever he tells you." This is, of course, the best advice anyone can ever give to someone else in regard to Jesus.

Notice what Mary has done here: she has put her Son in a position to act by publicly raising expectations that he would, and she has disposed those around him to cooperate with him in whatever way he says. While it's not our practice, one can hardly read this and blame Catholics for praying to Mary to intercede for them, because she does appear to have known how to get her Son to intervene even when he might have been reluctant to do so. At the end of the episode, we read: "Jesus performed this, the first of his signs, in Cana of Galilee and he showed forth his glory, and his disciples believed in him" (John 2:11). Within the story of John's Gospel, it is Mary who launches Jesus into the active revelation of his glory that would culminate in his crucifixion, the hour of his glorification.

Joseph and Mary raised four sons and several daughters alongside Jesus. Scripture hasn't left us any testimony to their growing-up years, but can you imagine what it was like for James or the other siblings in that household? "Why can't you be more like your brother?" "Give me a break, Mom; I'm sick and tired of being compared to Mr. Perfect over there!" According to John's Gospel, there were indeed some hard feelings between Jesus and his half-brothers in the early period of Jesus' ministry. Matthew and Mark tell of an episode in which Jesus radically redefined his family—a word that has given comfort and encouragement to millions of disciples but that was no doubt difficult for Jesus' blood relations to hear:

> [Jesus] was still speaking to the crowds. ... Someone told him, "Look, your mother and your brothers are standing outside, wanting to speak to you." ... Jesus replied, "Who is my mother, and who are my brothers?" And pointing to his disciples, he said, "Here are my mother and my brothers! For whoever does the will of my Father in heaven is my brother and sister and mother." (Matt 12:46–50 NRSV)

I can only imagine that it was painful for Mary to hear about Jesus' response; it was probably disappointing that, by all accounts, he stayed inside the house teaching and did *not* break away to talk to his blood relations. This was another occasion for Mary to die a little more to herself and to her own expectations for what her life would be like. She—like all of us, especially those who have close relationships within their natural families—was challenged to accept Jesus' vision of a much larger family, one whose claims superseded even the claims of one's natural family. It is important for us to recognize both this challenge *and* the fact that

Mary and her other children, insofar as we know, did come to embrace Jesus' vision of family—the family that would be formed by faith, by his blood—and thus remained part of Jesus' family and a vitally important part of that larger family that Jesus was calling together.

Of course, we all know where we will find Mary just a few years later, at the end of Jesus' ministry, for the sake of which he left the construction business and a rooted life in Nazareth.

> Meanwhile, standing near the cross of Jesus were his mother, and his mother's sister, Mary the wife of Clopas, and Mary Magdalene. When Jesus saw his mother and the disciple whom he loved standing beside her, he said to his mother, "Woman, here is your son." Then he said to the disciple, "Here is your mother." And from that hour the disciple took her into his own home. (John 19:25–27 NRSV)

This scene is deeply etched in Catholic piety, immortalized in a poem quite unfamiliar to most of us but well known to any Catholic, the Stabat Mater.

> At the Cross her station keeping,
> stood the mournful Mother weeping,
> close to her Son to the last.
> Through her soul, His sorrow sharing,
> all His bitter anguish bearing,
> now at length the sword has passed.

The echo of old Simeon's prediction some thirty years before Mary came to this moment is clearly heard in the poem at this point.

There were many things not to like about Mel Gibson's *Passion of the Christ*, but one thing I very much did like was the attention given to Mary during those terrible twenty-four hours—how, despite the fact that her own heart was breaking, she remained present, giving all her strength to her Son, showing him a loving face in the midst of a mocking mob, reminding him that he was not alone. However many liberties Gibson might have taken with this, that had to be the message, at least, that Jesus received when he saw his mother close by him from his cross. From the cross, Jesus gives his mother over to the care of the "beloved disciple." Mary would have to live the rest of her natural life without enjoying a natural relationship with her eldest son. It henceforth would be the spiritual relationship with the risen and ascended Christ that we all have the possibility of enjoying.

* * *

On the other side of the resurrection and ascension of her Son, we see Mary—for the last time in Scripture—there in the upper room with Jesus' eleven disciples plus the newly chosen twelfth, with the women who had accompanied and helped to support Jesus and his disciples' ministry, with Jesus' half-brothers, and about a hundred other devoted followers (Acts 1:13–15). She is surrounded by, and part of, that larger family that Jesus embraced—those committed to doing the will of Jesus' Father in heaven. The descent of the Holy Spirit upon those hundred and twenty disciples in the upper room, the event we celebrate on the day of Pentecost, is counted as the birth of the church. But just as Jesus was born of divine *and* human parentage, it might also be fair to think of Mary, in that upper room, in the midst of the family that she, too, helped birth by virtue of her humble submission to God's will, her willingness to endure reproach to accomplish God's purposes, her giving up of her own dreams and expectations to embrace and support Jesus' mission, and her steadfastness in standing by Jesus in love even when the sword was piercing her own heart. She proved herself a fitting mother *for* God's Son and, in so doing, shows us much about being fitting disciples *of* God's Son.

4

"Prepare Him Room" (Christmas)

Luke 2:1–7; Titus 2:11–14

One of the most poignant images from that first Christmas is the detail from Luke's Gospel that, when Mary "gave birth to her firstborn son," she "laid him in a feeding trough, because there was no room for them in the inn" (Luke 2:7). Think of every nativity set you have ever seen. Like the shepherds who were given this very sign by the angel, we recognize that we're looking at the baby Jesus—at a nativity scene—because the baby is lying in that most unconventional crib, a manger, an animal's feeding trough. In hindsight, it was most prophetic that there should be no room for Jesus to be born in a proper house or in the Bethlehem "B and B" for it would *always* be a struggle for us mortal men and women to make room for Jesus to come in, to take on flesh among us, to take on flesh within us.

And so the Son of God is born in the corner of some stable, quite possibly in the company of the livestock for whom that was a proper home. Now I don't think that the innkeepers of Bethlehem are much to be blamed. According to Luke, there was a great deal of movement among the population of Israel that month. Heads of households that had moved away from their ancestral towns were traveling back to those towns in droves to be registered there, and the supply of hospitality—no doubt *throughout* Israel—was simply exhausted by the unusual demand. Imagine that by some terrible scheduling fluke every high school and college in this country held its graduations and reunions on exactly the same weekend. A lot of people would find that there was no room for them in the local inns and guesthouses.

Indeed, one could say that a particular innkeeper or some other resident did the best that he could for Joseph and his pregnant wife, at least opening up his barn to them and affording them what shelter was available. He had no idea who it was that Mary was carrying. Doing the best he could under the crowded conditions no doubt seemed like enough—perhaps more than enough.

You and I, however? We can hardly excuse ourselves today for not doing better to make room for Jesus. On this side of his marvelous acts, which showed how God was with him—his acts of healing, his deliverance of those possessed, his raising even of the recently deceased—on this side of his crucifixion, resurrection from the dead, and ascension into heaven, which announce as with trumpets who this man is in the hierarchy of God's kingdom, we cannot treat him as did that ancient innkeeper, leading Mary and Joseph to the stable. The extent to which we *do* make room for Jesus, clearing out the spaces at the center of our lives for him, and the extent to which we do *not* make room for Jesus, ushering him out back to the margins of our lives—these are the markers that show God how much or how little we value God's grace when it shows up.

* * *

In a letter to his junior partner, Titus, the apostle Paul gives us one of the most compact and incisive statements about the significance of Jesus' birth as well as clear guidance on making room for Jesus.

> The grace of God showed up, bringing deliverance for all people, training us so that, by renouncing ungodliness and this-worldly desires, we might live soberly and justly and piously in the present age, while awaiting the blessed hope—even the appearing of the glory of our great God and Savior Jesus Christ, who gave himself on our behalf in order that he might redeem us from every lawless deed and purify a people for his own special possession, a people who are fanatical about doing good. (Titus 2:11–14)

God's favor, God's gift, "showed up," "revealed itself," "appeared on the scene." This is at the heart of the miracle of Christmas. The birth of Jesus, God the Son appearing on the scene in human flesh, is the precise moment when "the grace of God showed up" in a way that would forever change how God and human beings related. Human beings had alienated themselves from God—the gentiles by ignoring their Creator, putting other gods at the center of their lives, distorting and defacing their lives and relationships as a result (see Rom 1:18–32); the Jews by not honoring God through obeying his law, through not putting love for God and neighbor above all else (see Rom 2:17–29). But instead of giving up on human beings and letting loose his anger on us as we deserved, God does something completely unexpected and unbelievably generous: God invests himself in a new and marvelous way in the very human beings who had dishonored him by not making room for him who had created them—him who had given them whatever room in this world they themselves enjoyed (see Rom 5:1–11).

"The grace of God showed up" with a purpose: to bring deliverance—salvation—for all people. This purpose is captured in the very name that the angel commanded the Christ child be given—"You will call his name 'Jesus,' for he will save his people from their sins" (Matt 1:21). In the first instance, Paul no doubt has in mind deliverance from the *final* consequences of our sins—God's wrath, God's satisfaction of his honor that his creatures had trampled, holding them accountable and punishing them as their shameless affronts merit. But Paul also hints here at deliverance from the *immediate* consequences of our sins as well—the very disorder into which our lives had fallen, the personal, relational, and systemic dysfunction that becomes its own prison, its own hell, for the sinners who help to create and sustain it.

How does God bring about this deliverance? Paul may surprise us here, because he doesn't jump at once to a phrase like "by dying for our sins" or some such thing that Christ did on our behalf. Instead, he talks about this deliverance coming about as God changes us through God's training (or, perhaps better, retraining) us. God's grace manifests itself here first and foremost by educating us in how to live so as to give God our Redeemer at last the room that God our Creator has always deserved in our lives. Jesus, who was above all else a teacher, provided and continues to provide this training in the instructions that he gave and that have been preserved for us in the Gospels. His apostles provided further training as they sought to shape communities of disciples that would shape each individual disciple into a reflection of the mind and heart that was in Jesus, leaving us a record of this in Acts, the Epistles, and Revelation. The Holy Spirit, our personal trainer in righteousness and God-centered living, continues to provide this training to all who make room to hear and follow his promptings.

There is indeed a lot to clear out of our lives if we are to make room for Christ, if we are to give now to Christ the space he merits in our lives. Paul speaks of God's grace training us to "renounce ungodliness and this-worldly desires." When you hear the word "ungodliness," don't think immediately only of the most salacious self-indulgent or self-destructive activities. The word simply names the absence in a person's life of giving God the concern and attention that God merits. It is as much a lack of living reverently as it is living irreverently. And, as such, it catches quite a few more of us in the mirror it holds up. Similarly, "this-worldly desires" aren't all about excessive drinking, recreational drugs, and illicit sex. Paul is again naming a much broader slice of what occupies us, what pushes God out, what takes up so much room in our lives that there isn't room for him. We spend a lot of our limited time going after what this world offers, enjoying it, distracting ourselves with it, passing the time with it, and getting entangled in it, such that there's hardly any room *left* for God. If we were to be honest with ourselves, many of us would probably have to admit to fitting him in to the margins of our weeks—a Sunday morning here, maybe an evening there. And so Christ is back in the feeding trough, the manger, because there's no room for him in the house where we live most of our lives.

God's grace seeks to train us to renounce our lack of concern for the God who showed us such great concern. God's grace seeks to train us to renounce our attachments to, and investments in, the things that push God out of the room, to stop saying to God, when we give hours of our attention to distractions that will not leave us any better for having engaged them, "No, I want *this* more; I am drawn to *that* more; I need *this* more; I value *that* more; I expect, from *this*, more."

* * *

Keep the miracle of Christmas before your eyes, ruminate upon the love that God showed you here, by taking on our flesh and blood so as to share our human nature, to live and die as one of us, to reconcile us to himself, and grace will train you by awakening gratitude and teaching you how to live out that gratitude in living for God. This child was born, Paul goes on to say, to redeem us from "every lawless act" so that we might be pure, so that we might be fully Christ's own. By purifying us from our past sins, he makes room in us and in our lives to possess us fully, to make us fully his. Let gratitude train you to return the favor, to make more room for Christ indeed to be born in you, to grow in you, to raise *you* to the full stature that Christ attained (Gal 2:19–21).

If we allow God's grace thus to train us, we will find ourselves living, as our passage from Titus tells us, "soberly and justly and piously in the present age, while awaiting the blessed hope— even the appearing of the glory of our great God and Savior Jesus Christ":

- soberly, because we are living as people who are waking up to what's most valuable, most important;
- justly, because we are living in such a way as does what is right in God's sight, making room again and again for God-pleasing service because we are "fanatics for doing good";
- piously, because we are living in such a way as gives God, and what God merits, due attention, making appropriate room for God in our lives, in our selves, in our affections, desires, and commitments;
- soberly, again, because we know what is coming, for what we must continually prepare—our "blessed hope—even the appearing," the next "showing up, of the glory of our great God and Savior Jesus Christ."

Christ was content to be born in a stable and placed in a manger once, before we knew who he was. No longer. How will you clear out the very best place for him, the most central, the most honoring place for him in your hearts, in your homes, in that complex of activities from morning to night to the next morning that make up our lives? This Christmas, indeed, let *every* heart prepare him room. Amen.

5

"Living into Baptism" (Baptism of Our Lord)

Matthew 3:1–18; Romans 6:1–14

66 **I**n those days, John the Baptizer—John the Immerser—showed up, proclaiming in the Judean wilderness, saying: 'Repent—change your hearts and lives—because the kingdom of heaven has drawn near' " (Matt 3:1-2). What was John up to, dunking people in the Jordan River? Just as John himself appears to have one foot in the Old Testament, showing up in Elijah's camel-hair garment, and one foot in the New Testament, calling for readiness for a new visitation of God, so his immersion was something distinct both from the ritual baths of the old covenant and the baptism of the new covenant, with which we would identify.

Immersing oneself into water as a means of purifying oneself was routine in first-century Judea. One finds one or more smallish pools—each with a staircase leading down into the water that filled the pool to about chest level—in site after archaeological site. Such a pool is called a *mikveh* in Hebrew, and these were used regularly for ritual immersion, a kind of artificial replacement for the "living water" of a river, which was harder to access in most parts of Judea. They are often to be found in the houses of priestly families, who tended to be quite careful to observe the instructions in the law of Moses concerning dissipating everyday pollutions, or adjacent to synagogues throughout Israel. One would walk down into the *mikveh*; once at the bottom of the basin, kneel so as to immerse oneself completely; and then ascend from the basin. A number of these pools even had a short dividing wall built into the staircase (pictured), such that one could be sure to descend unclean on one side of the steps and ascend clean on the other half of the steps.

A person could contract uncleanness in many ways—touching a carcass, touching anything touched by a woman during her period, experiencing a seminal emission, having contact with someone who had any one of a variety of skin conditions or discharges, and the like. We shouldn't think of these concerns

as health issues either on the part of the Lawgiver or the Jews who were attentive to these matters. However, our own anxiety about who touched the bathroom door handle before us, whether he or she washed before doing so, and whether we should use a paper towel to open the door for ourselves and reach for our hand sanitizer shortly after do reflect a similar mental dynamic. The point of ritual cleansing was to immerse yourself so as to

be restored to a state of ritual cleanness or purity, such that you would not contribute to multiplying pollution in the holy land that the holy God had chosen for his dwelling.

It was particularly important to perform such an immersion prior to entering the temple precincts. The removal of all such defilement was essential before encountering the holy God, into whose presence one simply does not carry pollution, lest one risk God's holiness breaking out to consume the polluted one or the holy God withdrawing from the temple. Thus one finds *mikvaoth* in abundance in the priests' buildings and in the open spaces all around the temple in Jerusalem. The city was also equipped with massive pools, each of which probably functioned as a public *mikveh* serving the thousands upon thousands of residents and pilgrims that came to the temple each day—not to mention the tens of thousands upon tens of thousands that flooded the city during annual festivals like Passover and the Feast of Booths. The pool of Siloam (pictured)—famous for its role in the story of Jesus' healing of the man who had been born blind in John 9, only one edge of which has been uncovered—is one such pool. Another is the pool of Bethesda, the site of another healing miracle of Jesus, recorded in John 5.

*   *   *

All this is to say that the idea of being immersed in a body of water in connection with removing pollution for the sake of preparing oneself to encounter God would have been quite familiar to everyone who went out to the Jordan River to be immersed by John. But John's baptism—the immersion that John performed upon people—was also distinctive in some important respects.

Most obviously, John is immersing people for an encounter with God, but far from Jerusalem, its temple, and its establishment. "Prepare to meet God," but not *there*. God is indeed going to show up in a powerful and epoch-making way, but not *there*. "Prepare a spiritual highway for God to use as God comes to visit us," out *here*, in the margins of Judea, out here by the river. If John had preached and immersed in one of those large pools surrounding the Temple Mount, I doubt he would have had his head handed to him by the authorities.

John was also clearly not concerned merely with ritual purity. He called people to come to *this* immersion ready to change their hearts and their lives. This is, indeed, how the Common English Bible consistently translates the word that the NRSV renders "repent": "Change your hearts and lives!" (Matt 3:2 CEB). Your security before God isn't in claims about the past—"Don't presume to say 'We have Abraham as our father' " (Matt 3:9) and think that everything's therefore all right between you and God. Show in your lives that your repentance is real, that you've left loveless, unrighteous, mean-spirited ways behind you.

As far as we can tell, unlike the routine and repeated immersions performed throughout Judea and Galilee, John immersed people once in preparation for encountering God, in preparation for God's epoch-making intervention. This was a decisive cleansing looking forward to a decisive act of God showing up.

And so Jesus shows up at the Jordan to be baptized by his cousin John.

We remember this event each year on the Sunday after Epiphany for two reasons. First, Jesus' showing up is the manifestation for which John was waiting and for which he had been preparing the people in his call to a change of heart and life and his washing away of their pollutions. John recognizes this as he expresses his discomfort with being the one to immerse Jesus, preferring that Jesus should immerse—and thus cleanse and prepare—him. Second, God shows up as well to give Jesus an unparalleled endorsement: "This is my beloved Son, in whom I am well pleased" (Matt 3:17).

The Son of God who identified with us by sharing our flesh and blood thought it proper, now living in our flesh and blood, also to identify with John's immersion and with those who came responding to John's call, even as Jesus took up John's proclamation: "Repent, for the kingdom of heaven is drawing near!" (Matt 4:17). Indeed (Jesus would declare), God is visiting God's people and God's world in an epoch-changing way; indeed, the time for a change of heart and life is now; indeed, a decisive change is happening in history that calls for a decisive change in people's lives.

But the baptism that John offered, and the baptism that Jesus underwent, is not the baptism into which you and I were immersed. John called people to change their hearts and lives and to purify themselves in baptism prior to and in preparation for God's epoch-making intervention; the Christian church, beginning with the apostles calling those first thousands at the Feast of Pentecost, calls people to an immersion on the far side of, and in response to, God's epoch-making intervention—the death and resurrection of his Son, Jesus. The first episode in Acts 19 gives an early testimony to this difference, as Paul encounters believers who had only been baptized by John—whom he now baptizes in the name of Jesus and into the transforming power of his death and resurrection, with the result that the Holy Spirit descends upon those disciples in a powerful way.

In our reading from Paul's Letter to the Romans, we hear a very early sermonette on the meaning of baptism as the rite of entrance into the Christian church or, better, the rite of initiation into the baptismal life. In these paragraphs, Paul seeks to answer a basic question: Is God's grace toward us in Christ merely supposed to inoculate us against the consequences of our sins, or is it supposed to utterly transform our lives?

Some people in Paul's world have misunderstood his message and caricatured his preaching as a result. Earlier in Romans, Paul writes: "If my unrighteousness serves to establish God's righteousness, what should we say? Why not do wicked things so that good things can come of it? This is what some people slanderously claim that we are preaching" (Rom 3:5, 8). I often wonder how Paul himself would react to what many have made of Paul's gospel—a cheap grace that demands no change of life, no giving back to Jesus a life for a life. Paul himself, after all, gives voice to a very different vision:

> What are we to say, then? Shall we persist in sinning in order that grace may become even more abundant? Heck, no! We who have *died* to sin—how will we go on living in

it? Or don't you realize that as many of us as were baptized into Christ Jesus were baptized into his death? So we
were buried with Christ through baptism into his death
in order that, just as Christ rose from the dead through
the Father's glory, so we also might walk in a new kind
of life? (Rom 6:1–4)

You might hear this and think, "Well, to be honest, I've had very
little trouble continuing to sin. If I'm actually *dead* to sin, I'm
surprised at how active our relationship—sin's and mine—has
remained over the years." But our baptism and the availability of
the Holy Spirit *has* changed that relationship significantly. The
relationship is awkward now. We might occasionally hang out
together, sin and I, but the spark has gone out of our friendship.
Or it's like that shirt that, as soon as we put it on, we're sorry
we took it off the hanger, because it just doesn't fit right or look
right or feel comfortable any more.

What we're bumping up against here is the tension between
description and prescription in Paul's letters (as, indeed, in the
work of other New Testament writers). In one breath, they declare
what God has accomplished in us; in the next breath, they instruct
us to live up to what God has accomplished, as if to make the potential God has created in and for us real and actual or to let God's gift
to us and working within us have its full effect. We must live into
what God has done for us.

And so Paul declares: "Our former self was crucified with
him in order that the body of sin might be eliminated—in order
that we might no longer serve Sin as its slaves" (Rom 6:6). "Our
former self" isn't a pretty sight. It's greedy, jealous, angry; it
thinks and speaks ill of others, especially when they get in our
way or do something we don't happen to like; it acts viciously to
protect its own interests. In other words, it lives quite far away

from loving our neighbor as ourselves, from looking out for the other person's interests before our own, from reflecting Christ's heart in our own.

Jesus' death and resurrection are not just acts that he undertook on our behalf; they have become events in which we are invited to participate, and this is at the core of our baptism. Just as Jesus died and, having died, was no longer liable to death, since his mortal life was over, "in the same way, count yourselves also dead where sin is concerned"; just as Jesus now lives an entirely new kind of life in God's power, the resurrected life, "in the same way, count yourselves ... alive in Christ Jesus where God is concerned" (Rom 6:11). We join ourselves to Christ in his death, which means that we keep putting our old self, with its impulses and drives, behind us as something "dead to us," for Christ's death on our behalf has made this very thing possible for us. We join ourselves to Christ in his resurrection, which means that we keep living from the "newness of life," the "new kind of life," that came into being in us by the spark of God's Holy Spirit and that God's Holy Spirit continues to breathe into greater and greater strength and presence within us.

> Let sin, therefore, no longer exercise authority in your mortal bodies, so as to make you obey its impulsive desires, nor continue to put your body parts at sin's disposal as its tools for unrighteous activity, but keep putting yourselves at God's disposal as those living on the other side of death and your body parts at God's disposal as his tools for righteous activity. (Rom 6:12–13)

This new person with which we clothe ourselves in baptism is beautiful: compassionate, kind, humble, patient, forbearing. In its relationships it exhibits the beauty of forgiveness, love, and harmony (see Col 3:12–17). The new person is Christ living in us and us living for Christ; to live this life is to be created anew by God, to become our "best self" in him.

Ultimately, it is our dying to the "former self" with Christ, who died for us, and our living from the "newness of life" nurtured by the Spirit, that, according to Paul, gives us reliable assurance about one day also living the resurrected life of Christ ourselves:

> For if we have become closely identified with the likeness of his death, we will also be closely identified with the likeness of his resurrection. … And if we died with Christ, we trust that we will also live together with him. (Rom 6:5, 8)

All of this Paul connects to the rite of baptism, a ritual act that mystically effects our participation in Christ's death and brings Christ to life within us—not because of anything special in this water, but because it has pleased God to act wherever this water is applied in his name and in the name of his Anointed One.

* * *

For baptism to be fully baptism, it must not cease its work when we leave the font. It must become more and more the mold that shapes our lives, until Christ lives in us and we live for Christ. It must become more and more the compass point from which we chart each day's course, until we follow the promptings of the Holy Spirit—that is, walk in newness of life—more naturally and readily than we follow our own desires. As Martin Luther once expressed, baptism is to become the garment which the disciple is to put on every day, each day putting the old person to death a little more and nurturing the new person toward maturity.[1]

1. Adapted from Martin Luther, *The Large Catechism*, translated by Robert H. Fischer (Philadelphia: Fortress, 1959), 90.

This union with Christ in his death and resurrection is a spiritual grace continually held out to us in our baptism. It is a precious gift from God, allowing us ever to leave behind whatever is destructive to human relationships, to community, and ultimately to ourselves and to move into a life with God and with one another that releases God's love into this world and preserves us with Christ for eternity. And so the church perpetually reminds us: "Remember your baptism, and be thankful."[2]

2. This liturgical formula is used in services of baptismal renewal, such as the one found in *The United Methodist Hymnal* (Nashville: Abingdon Press, 1989), 35-37.

6

"A Necessary Spoiler" (Transfiguration)

Mark 9:2–9; 2 Peter 1:12–19

Spoilers. You *have* to hate them. Movies depend upon unforeseen plot twists to be effective entertainment. Screenwriters and directors go out of their way to make sure that the steps of the plot are revealed at the right time; in the best movies, they make sure that dramatic tension is allowed to build to the very breaking point before a dramatic resolution or revelation occurs. Imagine how much less effective *When Harry Met Sally* would have been if we had seen an aged Billy Crystal and Meg Ryan as one of the old married couples being interviewed at the beginning of the film instead of at the very end, having wondered for two hours if they would *ever* finally get together? Or if we saw Bruce Willis's widow standing by his graveside ten minutes into *The Sixth Sense*, or if the little kid had said, a half hour into the film, "I see dead people ... like you, for instance"? Or if, when Luke Skywalker asked old Ben Kenobi twenty minutes into *Star Wars: A New Hope*, "You knew my father?" Ben replied, "Yes, a great Jedi that Anakin. Pity he turned to the dark side and now goes by 'Darth Vader.'"

But, when it comes to life, we desperately want spoilers. We want to hear an authoritative voice speak the words, "We're definitely going to beat this cancer; it will just take a few rounds of radiation and it'll be all behind you." Or, "Things are going to work out just fine for your daughter—two years from now she'll be a new person with this addiction completely behind her." Or, "I've already seen the two of you reconciled again with all of this mess behind you; it will just take a few months of work to get there." Sometimes we would give just about anything for a spoiler, to get us through the hard times in which we find ourselves, to give us the assurance we crave that the outcome will be good. If we had *that*, then maybe, just maybe, we could persevere through the hard times and not give up along the way.

* * *

God appears to have decided that Jesus' inner core of disciples needed such a spoiler if they were going to press on, for that's essentially what we find here in this strange story of the transfiguration of Jesus. Things were getting a bit bumpy for them before we got to this mountaintop. Jesus had gathered his disciples around him, asking them about public perception of him and, finally, asking them about their own perception. Peter had boldly declared, "You are the Messiah!" In response to Peter's confession, Jesus tells them to keep it to themselves, because "the Son of Man must suffer many things and be rejected by the elders and chief priests and the scribes and be killed, and after three days rise again" (Mark 8:31). None of this, of course, was in *anyone's* messianic playbook, so Peter tries to set Jesus straight on what it really means to be the Messiah, earning Jesus' sharp rebuke: "Get behind me, Satan! You're not thinking God's thoughts, but merely human thoughts!" (Mark 8:33).

If that wasn't difficult enough, Jesus followed this up with an on-the-spot teaching to the crowds about what it would mean to follow such a Messiah as he was: "If any want to follow me, let them deny themselves, pick up their crosses, and follow me. For as many as want to preserve their lives will lose them, but as many as lose their lives for my sake and the sake of the gospel will be the ones to preserve them" (Mark 8:34–35). Such an invitation would probably have sounded like the equivalent of this: "The first person to give away all his or her money will be the richest of all. Ready? Set? Go!"

But Jesus is clearly very serious about this claim, for he follows it up with an urgent warning: "Whoever is ashamed of me and of my words in front of this sinful and adulterous brood, the Son of Man will also be ashamed of him or her whenever he comes in the glory of his Father with the holy angels" (Mark 8:38). Whoever does not own this Jesus, even if following him means putting reputation and life on the line, Jesus will not own on some mysterious future date after he himself is ... put to death. What? Isn't that what he said was going to happen to him? Why am I following *him*, exactly?

I think God gave a few key disciples a bit of a break at this point. They were being asked to swallow a whole lot, and they needed something to help them see that, yes, Jesus' vision for his own messiahship was heading somewhere glorious. Yes, Jesus did have a place in God's plan that was every bit as central and exalted as he had suggested with that last bit about loyalty to him now, on *this* side of history, being determinative for one's well-being at some future point when Jesus would come again in glory. Yes, following this Jesus to the end and beyond did make sense as a sound investment of one's life. The transfiguration was a spoiler, but it was a necessary one.

Peter, James, and John got a glimpse of the glory that Jesus, as the eternal Son, had had with the Father before his incarnation; they got a glimpse of the glory that Jesus would have, not just on the far side of his resurrection but on the far side of his ascension and, ultimately, at his coming again as Lord and Judge. This was the glorified Christ that Paul would encounter as he rode off to Damascus to persecute the Jesus cult that was eroding loyalty to the covenant of Israel, as he saw it. This was the glorified Christ that John would see on the island of Patmos as he entered into the visionary experience that would eventually yield the book of Revelation. It is no doubt because of this that we always celebrate the transfiguration at the close of the season of Epiphany. Short of the second coming itself, it is the ultimate epiphany, the ultimate revelation of Jesus' glory, within the story of the Gospels.

It's a strange story—but hold on, it gets stranger. The disciples do not see Jesus alone in this glory; they see Moses and Elijah showing up to talk with him. Bear in mind that, according to the Old Testament, Elijah is never said to have died, exactly. When the time came for his prophetic ministry to be over, a flaming chariot whisked him away to the divine realm. It is because of this distinctive departure that later Jews expected to see him again, prior to God's decisive interventions in history. The closing words of the prophet Malachi, in fact, are these: "Look! I will send the prophet Elijah to you before the great and terrible day of the Lord arrives. He will turn the hearts of the parents toward their children and the hearts of children to their parents, lest I come and strike the land with a curse" (Mal 4:5–6). In the final chapter of Deuteronomy, we read that Moses died (Deut 34:5–6), so his availability to appear here is harder to explain. Nevertheless, the symbolism of these two men coming to speak with Jesus is unmistakable—the giver of the law and the foremost of the prophets were conversing with the One in whom both the Law and the Prophets would find their fulfillment.

Luke says that the topic was Jesus' departure—in Greek, the word is *exodos*—"which he was about to accomplish in Jerusalem" (Luke 9:31). Mark, however, doesn't say anything about the topic of their conversation. This was not part of the story that was important to him, and he leaves it to his readers to speculate, if they wish. He pushes ahead to the climax, where a cloud—the visual symbol of God's own presence settling down on a place—covers the six figures, and God pronounces with his own voice: "This is my Son, my beloved one—*listen* to him" (Mark 9:7). In Mark's Gospel, the first time the divine voice speaks, it is to Jesus at his baptism: "You are my Son, my beloved; in you I am well pleased" (Mark 1:11). This is a second divine authorization of Jesus' teaching, this time with his inner circle unmistakably hearing the voice. To listen to Jesus *is* to obey the voice of God.

How strange, Jesus' command to the three *not* to share the experience with anyone else until after his resurrection. It must have stunk to have been Peter's brother Andrew! "So, what went on up there on the mountain? Anything interesting?" "Sorry, can't really talk about it. Inner circle stuff." We are more aware while reading Mark's Gospel, specifically, how intent Jesus is that nothing should get in the way of his giving his life as a ransom for many on Calvary. The time for talking about his divine glory is *after* that work is done.

How strategic, Jesus' command to the three not to share the experience with anyone else until after his *resurrection*. Even though they will continue to have trouble understanding, Jesus creates a mental hook for them: this awesome manifestation of his glory, this fleeting lifting of the veil that hid his divinity from view, should keep them looking forward to what would happen at the end of those long three days after he was nailed up on a cross and died.

Now, I have to admit that I am personally jealous of Peter, James, and John. I'm jealous of Paul with his Damascus road experience, and I'm jealous of John the prophet, who was the last New Testament author to see the glorified Christ, to be visited by him and to encounter him. I have often wished—I have sometimes prayed—for such an encounter. I think it would go a long way toward burning off the mist of doubt, the reluctance to commit *all* the way.

But I'm reminded that even such a vision doesn't resolve everything—it certainly didn't for Peter, James, and John in Mark's Gospel. Not long after this episode we find James and John taking Jesus aside and asking him to allow them to take seats at his right and left hand in his glory. They understood the coming exaltation of Jesus just fine and saw it as a source of personal advantage to them both—clearly Peter was the only real competition they had to beat out. But they didn't yet understand what it meant to follow Jesus *now*, on the way to glory, that whoever wishes to be most distinguished among Jesus' disciples must most distinguish himself or herself as a servant of others, just as "the Son of Man came not to be served, but to serve—and to give his life as a ransom for many" (Mark 10:45). The vision of Jesus transformed, radiant with the glory that had been and would again be his, didn't help Peter in the courtyard of the high priest. It didn't embolden him when Jesus was on trial for his life to stand by his master and own him as his friend and teacher, as a man who had done nothing worthy of being put on trial, as a man whom God himself had invested with authority and called his Son.

Through that long Saturday, however, and through that long night into Sunday, did Peter, did James and John, remember their experience with Jesus on the mountain? Did they look at one another in that room behind the bolted doors, and did they remember that experience that only the three of them had that day? Did they remember that they couldn't tell their brothers and sisters in that upper room until after Jesus' resurrection? His *resurrection!* Did it keep them looking forward, daring to hope that there would be an "after" the resurrection?

After the resurrection, we can well imagine that the memory of this event became even more important. "He told us all along; he even showed us; now we experience him risen—we're not giving up now, no matter what."

*   *   *

If you were to read just Romans through Revelation—the back half of the New Testament—and write down everything we know about Jesus' life from those twenty-two texts, it would surprise you how little you would write down. But the transfiguration would be one of those events, referred to in some detail in 2 Peter:

> For we didn't make known to you the power and coming of our Lord Jesus Christ on the basis of following cleverly invented myths, but on the basis of having been eyewitnesses of his majesty—for we were with him on the holy mountain and we ourselves heard the voice that was borne from heaven when he received honor and glory from God the Father and the voice was borne from the Majestic Glory to him: "This is my Son, my Beloved, in whom I am well pleased." (2 Pet 1:16–18)

In this letter, the apostle Peter is preparing for *his* departure, his *exodos* (2 Pet 1:15), specifically preparing those Christian communities for which he feels responsible to carry on in the same assurance after his departure. The letter responds to a challenge being voiced against a core conviction of the faith—"Where is this promised 'coming' of his, for ever since our fathers died everything has gone on the same way since the beginning of creation?" (2 Pet 3:4). Peter offers his eyewitness testimony to the transfiguration—the revelation of Jesus' glory on the mountain—as evidence against this challenge.

Mark had also understood the transfiguration as a sign, a foretaste, a spoiler of the second coming. Just prior to this episode, Jesus had said: "There are some standing here who will not taste death before they see the kingdom of God coming in glory" (Mark 9:1). Mark understood this to be fulfilled in the transfiguration, the next episode he relates—and the only episode in the story of Jesus up to this point that he connects to the preceding one with a precise timeline ("*Six days later*, Jesus took Peter and James and John and led them up to a high mountain," Mark 9:2). Second Peter understands the transfiguration in precisely the same way—a visionary experience of Jesus at his second coming. It was an experience that—for Peter, James, and John, at least—made the prophetic word more certain for them; the apostolic testimony can do the same for us.

*   *   *

We confess that the death and resurrection of Jesus occurred just as Jesus foretold; if we did not, we would have little reason to gather in a church on Sunday morning rather than linger in bed or chill at Starbucks or kick around the mall. The transfiguration gives us additional assurance that the story will yet unfold as Jesus promised—that, as we confess in our creeds, "he will come again in glory to judge the living and the dead, and his kingdom will have no end." It is a conviction meant not to remain in our heads or merely to find expression on our lips but to shape our entire life. As Peter will express it at the close of his second letter, looking ahead to the cataclysmic coming of Christ that would usher in the new creation:

> Since all these things are thus slated for destruction, what kind of people, then, are you obliged to be, awaiting and hastening the coming of the day of God in holy conduct and reverent piety! (2 Pet 3:11–12a)

I don't know that Peter would have been all that surprised to learn that the end would still not have come almost two thousand years later. He almost anticipated this as he wrote:

> Don't let this one thing escape you, beloved, namely that one day is as a thousand years to the Lord, and a thousand years as a single day. The Lord does not delay in fulfilling his promise, as some people reckon a delay, but he is patient where you're concerned, not wishing for any to perish, but for all to come to repentance. (2 Pet 3:8–9)

It is perhaps not accidental that the Sunday of the Transfiguration immediately precedes the beginning of Lent. Taking seriously the promise of Christ's return and the prospect of encountering him as the Judge of all things, and rightly understanding every day that he delays as a gift to us to prepare ourselves *and* our neighbors more fully, naturally leads us to examine our lives more closely, to repent of all that does not reflect "holy conduct and reverent piety," and to devote ourselves more fully to all those things and only those things that will leave us unashamed at his coming in glory.

7

"The Divine Source Code" (Lent)

Matthew 4:1–11; Hebrews 4:12–16

*C*omputers and the internet have not only changed the way we access information in and do business with the world around us—they have changed the way we think about our interactions with other human beings, even the way we think about the way we think. They have provided us with a new realm of metaphors for our own mental processes and our social encounters. Consider the following snippets of conversation you might hear in a number of everyday settings:

"We need to get his *input* on this. I'll try to *interface* with him later this week."

"That's just not the way I'm *programmed.*"

"I don't think I have the *bandwidth* to deal with that on top of everything else right now."

"That's just a lot for me to *process* right now."

"It's about time to *reboot* the evangelism committee."

So, rather than fight the trend, I spent some time searching for an appropriate computer metaphor for the role that the Scriptures appear to have played in Jesus' formation prior to his encounter with the tempter in the desert—and, by extension, the role that the Scriptures ought to play in our ongoing formation if we are to share in his triumph over the tempter.

I landed upon the idea of "source code." Now, I'm not sufficiently computer-savvy to explain this in a nuanced fashion. Nevertheless, a program's source code is the version of the program that real-life programmers use to communicate to one another about the program and to outline its parameters and functions. It's the version of a computer program that human beings can actually read and fairly well understand. It is not yet the "machine code" version of the program that the inanimate computer will actually read, on the basis of which the program will actually run. The source code contains the essential information but also has to be "translated" to be put into practice in a computer's functioning.

Scripture speaks to us, for the most part, very clearly. It communicates very clearly God's vision for how we will live our lives together, for where we will fix our desires and aspirations, and even for how we will recognize whether the impulses that surface within us come from his Holy Spirit or from some other source. Of course, we still have to figure out which parts of it apply in particular situations; we still have to do the work of translating it from source code to machine code, from words on the sacred page to some real-time, real-world response that we are going to make in a given situation. But we can all read and, for the most part, understand quite well the details of the program God is seeking to install in each one of us as we, together with the Holy Spirit, do the real work of pushing the divine source code of Scripture into the machine code of our actual impulses and responses.

In Satan's encounter with Jesus in the Judean desert, Satan is trying to mess with Jesus' programming. He's trying to inject some subroutines that will actually cause the whole program to break down—"If X, then Y"; "If you're the Son of God, then ..." Jesus is so well-grounded in the word, however, that he recognizes and rejects these suggestions, these sidetracks, these viruses, and returns to that program that God has successfully put in place as Jesus has worked with, internalized, and continued to apply the divine source code.

*   *   *

The Judean desert is mercilessly hot. It's blindingly bright. It's bone dry. Forty days out there without food, going who knows how long between water sources, will break a person down to the level of his or her most basic instincts. It will show what a person is at the very core. So, of course, this is the point at which Satan decides to have a go at Jesus, when Jesus is broken down to his most vulnerable. And what does Satan ultimately encounter? Truly, the Word-made-flesh—not the weak flesh that he is accustomed to overthrowing, but flesh made strong by the Word, which has permeated and steeled it. He comes against Deuteronomy—the law of God—incarnate. Jesus may give expression to it in a parched, raspy voice, but it is Deuteronomy itself that speaks: "It is written, 'Human beings will not live on the strength of bread alone, but on the nourishment that comes from every word that proceeds from God's mouth' " (Matt 4:4; compare Deut 8:3); "It is written, 'You will not test the Lord your God' " (Matt 4:7; compare Deut 6:16); "It is written, 'The Lord your God is the one whom you will worship; him *only* will you serve' " (Matt 4:10; compare Deut 6:13).

The first and the last thing that I would have you take away from this story is how central this internalizing of Scripture was to Jesus' own success in staying on track, in continuing to move in line with the Father's program—and, if for him, how much more for us! In the story of Jesus' temptation we see the perfect embodiment of the psalmist's declaration: "I have hidden your word in my heart so that I might not sin against you" (Ps 119:15). Over the course of his first thirty years Jesus had devoted himself to the study of the Scriptures and to their implementation in his daily life. He had reprogrammed himself so that Scripture itself had become his operating system (to confuse the computer metaphor even further); when everything else was stripped away, the Scriptures and continuing to walk in line with the Scriptures was what was left. This disciplined internalization of God's word empowered Jesus—even here at his most vulnerable—to recognize whether the source of a suggestion was God or something other; his disciplined commitment to walk in line with God's promptings and God's alone, then, empower him to reject the suggestions.

During this season of Lent, take up the word with renewed interest and devotion. Read it; internalize it. As Jesus' half-brother James wrote in his letter, "Receive with meekness the implanted word that has the power to save your souls." He further admonishes, "Be doers of the word, and not merely hearers who deceive themselves" (Jas 1:21–22). Don't just read the divine source code; keep working diligently to implement it in your life, allowing it to shape your responses, your aspirations, your practices, your very instincts.

Now, I've read a lot of books by scholars interested in the "historical Jesus," and I can tell you that this particular episode doesn't fare too well when it comes to scholars trying to sift out the legends from the history. I think, however, that these scholars aren't being critical enough in regard to their own reading of the story. If we visualize this episode as involving Satan showing up in a black suit or, as in one movie version of the life of Jesus, as an alluring woman in a red dress, of course we're going to think of it as legend. But when does Satan *ever* actually show up like that? When does he not prefer to manifest himself as that thought that just occurs to you and then burrows in and seeks to take root?

So I see a famished Jesus looking at some nice round stones baking in the Judean sun and visualizing hot, fresh bread. *If you've got the power, why not satisfy that gnawing hunger inside you?* There's nothing particularly insidious about the suggestion; no one's going to get hurt if Jesus turns a few stones into bread—no one's even going to notice. But it's not just the content of the suggestion that's important; the *source* is also important. Why is Jesus out in the desert to begin with? To practice some miracles, or to learn to recognize and overcome demonic tests? Why is Jesus in this world to begin with? To satisfy his own cravings, or to do whatever it is that God prompts? Is it *God* telling Jesus to break his fast, or does the impulse come from some other source? For Jesus, the source of every impulse must be God. It's not just bread but the word spoken by God that gives a person genuine life.

There's a parishioner who has spoken to me often of Abraham Maslow's hierarchy of needs, suggesting that we need to care for people's physical needs, get them on a secure social footing, and thus put them in a position to be able to think about spiritual things and be receptive to the gospel. Maslow's theories seem essentially sound and defensible as a theory of human motivation, laying out what needs must be met before other, higher-order needs can move to the forefront of a human being's consciousness. The temptation story, however, gives me pause about it. What *are* our most fundamental needs, not merely as organisms, but as *creatures—created* organisms, *spiritual* organisms? Is Maslow's pyramid really just a manifestation of the demonic logic and prioritization of values that our society as a whole has internalized and now accepts as a given? I don't know, and I'm not really qualified to say. I've never known hunger, homelessness, lack of a social network—never really lacked *anything* on Maslow's pyramid. But we follow one who said:

> Don't be anxious, saying "What are we to eat?" or "What are we to drink?" or "How will we clothe ourselves?" *These* are the sorts of things the gentiles seek after. Don't be anxious, for your Father in heaven realizes that you need all these things. So, first and foremost, pursue his kingdom and righteousness, and all these things will be thrown in for you as well. (Matt 6:32–33)

How does Satan come to us, to impede our obedience to Jesus' setting of our priorities? Put the needs of your body first. Put the wants of your eyes and body first. Put the excessive cravings of your eyes and your pride and your body first. Make sure you satisfy your cravings, wants, and needs. And, sure, attend to God and to God's agenda for your life and your world once you've gotten those other things well in hand.

A very popular devotional periodical is entitled *Our Daily Bread*. It's a phrase from the Lord's Prayer, of course—"Give us this day our daily bread"—but it's also a reinterpretation of that phrase, suggesting that our most fundamental nourishment, even more fundamental than food, comes from meditation on God's word. This is, incidentally, why fasting has always remained so central and so valued a spiritual discipline, first in Jewish circles and then in Christian ones. It trains us to rethink our hierarchy of needs and decide which ones are truly fundamental, truly to be put first.

Satan really didn't have to physically convey Jesus to the highest corner of the Temple Mount enclosure to plant his next suggestion—and we ourselves don't have to be tempted to some crazy, suicidal act in order to be led to put God to the test. Similar suggestions plague us and our loved ones with merciless frequency. "If you love me, God, you'll heal this cancer"; "If you're *there*, God, you'll find me a job"; "If this promise of yours is true, you'll come through for me right now." When the cancer grows, or the job does not materialize, or God does not perform, the person walks away from God, having posed a test and having come to believe that God failed to pass the test—as if the dynamics of our relationship with God permitted us to pose such tests in the first place. No, Jesus had come to understand, God's promises in Scripture, like the one that Satan brought to his mind from Psalms ("God's angels will bear you up, lest you dash your foot against a stone," Ps 91:11-12), are not there to be fulfilled at *our* initiative and upon our demand but at *God's* initiative and upon his command. When God tells me to jump off the pinnacle of the temple, I can trust that his angels will bear me aloft. If it's just me wanting to see if God's promises are trustworthy, well, the *thud* will be loud and the splatter pattern wide.

The third exchange is probably a familiar temptation to many of us, though Satan generally approaches us more subtly—and far less generously. "Make sure you get your little piece of the kingdoms of the world and their glory. All it requires is your time, focus, and energy, and it will be yours. And, of course, if you've got any time or energy or inclination leftover, by all means worship God, cultivate the inner life, and serve him. But make sure you get these things first." To what extent, if we were to be truly honest with ourselves, have we set aside the commandment to "worship the Lord your God and serve him only" for the sake of getting what *we* want out of this world—trading in our first allegiance to God for a whole lot less than "all the kingdoms of the world and their splendor"?

*   *   *

Hebrews 4:12–16 offers an apt complement to the temptation story as a commentary both on the power of the word of God and the availability of help in the face of temptation. It begins thus:

> God's word is living and active and sharper than any two-edged sword, penetrating unto the splitting of soul from spirit, of joint from marrow, evaluating the thoughts and intentions of the heart—and there is no creature who can hide from his gaze, but all are naked with their throats laid bare before the eyes of him with whom is our reckoning. (Heb 4:12–13)

It is a fearsome series of images—standing with our throats exposed before the Judge who wields the power of a sword that is able to carve us up cleanly. But if we diligently engage the word of God now as *surgeon*, we will avoid encountering the word of God later as *executioner*.

It is interesting to me that one of the most fear-inspiring images in Hebrews is juxtaposed with one of the most confidence-inspiring:

> Since, then, we have a great high priest, one who has crossed through the heavens—Jesus, the Son of God—let us hold on to our confession. For we don't have a high priest who is unable to sympathize with our weaknesses, but one who has been tempted in every way like ourselves—only without sinning. Let us keep drawing

closer, then, to the throne of favor in order that we might receive mercy and find favor for timely help. (Heb 4:14–16)

The temptation story assures us that, indeed, "Jesus knows our every weakness."[1] He is able to feel sympathy for our weakness because he himself experienced our weakness, our vulnerability to temptation, our experience of being tested by life's changes and chances. Just as importantly, however, he is able to stand before God on our behalf, procuring God's mercy and favor for timely help, because he did not succumb to that weakness. When we are tempted—not just to do something grossly and overtly un-Christian but to give up on or fall short of doing what is quintessentially Christian—we can approach God's throne, the throne of favor, with boldness, confident that God will indeed show us mercy and supply us with all that is needful to persevere in the way of faithfulness and grateful service. Jesus will secure for us the help that we need to keep walking in line with God's word, to continue to work out, in the routines of our own lives, the intentions of the divine source code.

Now, of course, whether or not this sermon has been of any value at all will not be determined by the level of inspiration you might feel today. It will be determined by whether or not you open up the word—and open yourself up before and to the Word—tomorrow. I pray that we all, each one of us, will continue to seek out and to receive the word that God will implant more and more fully within us, unto the salvation of our souls—and unto the consistent defeat of the enemy of our souls.

1. From the hymn "What a Friend We Have in Jesus," written by Joseph M. Scriven.

8

"Letting in the Light" (Lent)

Psalm 139; 1 John 1:5–2:2

We grow up being taught that human beings have five senses—sight, smell, hearing, taste, and touch. We can lose one or more of these senses, but we can't naturally turn them on and off (save, of course, for closing our eyes). If we have them, they're on pretty much all the time. All of these senses pertain to our perception of phenomena in the natural, physical world.

The author of Psalm 139, however, bears witness to another sense, one that allows him to perceive a particular Phenomenon in the spiritual world—God. And what a remarkably keen sense of God this psalmist has! How vivid, how deeply personal, how *real* God is to him!

O Lord, you have searched me and known me.
You know when I sit down and when I rise up;
    you discern my thoughts from far away.
You search out my path and my lying down
    and are acquainted with all my ways.

Even before a word is on my tongue,
    O LORD, you know it completely.
You hem me in, behind and before,
    and lay your hand upon me. ...
Where could I go from your spirit?
    Where could I flee from your presence?
If I ascend to the skies, you're there;
    if I make my bed in the underworld, you're there.
If I take flight as the dawn
    and settle at the farthest western limits of the sea,
even there your hand would lead me,
    and your right hand would grasp me. (Ps 139:1–4,
        6–10, adapted from NRSV)

We may believe and confess that God is present everywhere; this psalmist expects to *bump into* God everywhere. We may confess that God is all-knowing and sees everything that happens under heaven; this psalmist lives in the awareness that God knows *all about him* and sees everything that might dart about in the creases of his brain or most hidden corners of his heart. He *feels* God's eyes upon him and penetrating him; he is intimately aware of God's intimate awareness of everything that has gone into making him who he has become, from the splitting of the first fertilized cell that was him in the womb.

*   *   *

This psalm asks each of us, first and foremost: Do you exercise this God-sense regularly? Do you give yourself time to *experience* the presence of God "hemming you in behind and before," to sense the hand of God resting upon you (Ps 139:5)? My ears are always open: I am constantly hearing the sounds around me. My nose is just about always open (allergy season excepted): I am constantly able to smell any new scent, for better or worse, that wafts my way. I wish that I could say that my sense of God was always open, that I was as constantly aware of God's presence as I'm aware of the sound if there's music playing or people talking or that I was as constantly aware of God's prompting as I'm aware of the first whiff of cookies baking. I wish that I could say that *my* sense of *God's* sense of *me* was always open, so that I have the benefit, in regard to everything that moves me or drives me in a given moment, of hearing God telling me, "Hold on there; that's not from me," or "Where's that coming from? Is there something there we should talk about?" The psalm, however, encourages me that we *can* become so aware—or, at the very least, a great deal *more* aware.

What the psalmist has given us is a prayer that can help each one of us quicken this God-sense a bit more. This is one of the many gifts of Scripture—the psalms and prayers that arose out of the experience of a distant ancestor in the faith can open us up to the same kind of experience as we use their words to focus our own minds, hearts, and spirits. And the goal of this psalm is not unfamiliar to many who frequently pray, in services of Holy Communion, a brief prayer that begins: "O God, unto whom all hearts are open, all desires known, and from whom no secrets are hidden." The prayer, like the psalm, doesn't open *God* up to us—it opens *us* up to God; it invites us to experience our own hearts, our own desires, our own secrets as they are laid open before God. It does so, moreover, with the same goal as our psalm. We ask, in that prayer, "Cleanse the thoughts of our hearts by the inspiration of your Holy Spirit, that we may perfectly love you and worthily magnify your holy Name."[1] The

---

1. *The Book of Common Prayer and Administration of the Sacraments and Other Rites and Ceremonies of the Church together with The Psalter or Psalms of David*

psalmist asks God, before whom he now stands fully aware of God's all-penetrating scrutiny:

> Search me, O God, and know my heart;
> test me and know my thoughts.
> See if there is any wicked way in me,
> and lead me in the way everlasting.
> (Ps 139:23–24 NRSV)

The psalmist invites us to keep coming with him before the God who knows us better by far than we know ourselves. And where the psalm ends, God's actual work with us begins. The silences and the conversations with God that *follow* the praying of this psalm are the ones in which we permit God to lay bare to our own gaze what we hide from ourselves, what we don't want to admit about ourselves—whether because it's never easy for us proud human beings to acknowledge that we are in the wrong about something, or because we've worked hard over long years to build up defenses against admitting something *about* ourselves *to* ourselves, or because it will mean necessary changes: "Search me, O God. ... See if there is any wicked leaning in me." Lay bare what hasn't yet been transformed by your Holy Spirit, and show me the path toward transformation even there.

* * *

Now, if you pray through this psalm at home, using it regularly to arrive at the same awareness of God that the psalmist himself expresses in the psalm, you're in for a bit of a shock when you get to verses 19–22. In the middle of this prayer celebrating

According to the use of the Episcopal Church (New York: The Church Hymnal Corporation, 1979), 355.

God's intimate knowledge of the one praying and God's happily inescapable presence and guiding hand, the psalm suddenly goes sideways:

> O that you would slay the wicked, O God!
>> Would that people of violence might be gone from
>>> me—
> those who speak of you with malice,
>> who rise up against you to do evil!
> Don't I hate those who hate you, O LORD?
>> Don't I abhor those who rise up against you?
> I hate them completely;
>> I count them among *my* enemies. (Ps 139:19–22)

Indeed, similar exclamations appear in several of the psalms. Very often these are purged from the reading or the reciting of the psalms in Christian worship, for they are deemed inappropriate in a community that has been charged by its Lord to "keep showing love to your enemies and keep praying for those who are persecuting you" (Matt 5:44). We often are embarrassed, frankly, by these exclamations in the psalms, even though few of us can claim never to have treasured such wishes in our hearts.

There are several ways to make sense of these declarations of hatred and prayers for the elimination of the wicked. We could view them as a declaration of absolute loyalty to God. The psalmist notably does not presume that his own personal enemies are God's enemies; rather, he declares that he will regard God's enemies as his own enemies as well. He is on the Lord's side against all who abuse God's honor.

We could view them as anguished expressions born of suffering deep injustice and oppression. I may not have suffered such significant injustice as to possess the right to pray before

God as this psalmist prays, but many people in our world *have* so suffered. I think of the helpless villagers with limbs hacked off by rebels in Sierra Leone as a standard practice in a terror campaign that lasted a decade. I think of the families of the Christian men lined up on their knees in orange suits and slaughtered like livestock by ISIS militants. I think of the villages full of families whose preteen daughters were abducted by Boko Haram to become brides with which to reward their soldiers. Those situations are not terribly unlike situations faced in ancient Israel during the Assyrian and Babylonian invasions, and I, for one, will not judge even the psalmist who cries out against Babylon: "Blessed is he who takes your little ones and dashes their heads against the rocks!" (Ps 137:9). Babylonians did as much in Jerusalem.

As for me, I view them as invitations—even as *warrants*—to be completely honest in God's presence. The rawness of the psalmists' expressions of their feelings before God encourages me to raw honesty in prayer. The psalmist is deeply aware that God knows already all that is on his heart, both that which is seemly for polite "church talk" and that which is ugly and unredeemed. And so the psalmist holds nothing back. He lays it all bare in prayer before God and before himself, owning those emotions and those wishes and putting them out there right in the open for God and for him to deal with together. If the emotions are unredeemed and the wishes ungodly, it's alright. We're not in danger of our angry prayers convincing God to do anything out of character for him, nor are we in danger of showing God a side of ourselves of which God was previously unaware. But if we own them, if we admit them to *ourselves* in God's presence, God may just work within us to set our hearts and desires back in order with his character. It's a mistake for us, when we pray, to try to show God only our "church face." God is already also quite aware of our backside, our darker side. We need to open up all of that before him in prayer as well, so as to let in his light.

Interestingly, it is immediately after his sideways step of declaring his hatred for God's enemies that the psalmist turns his prayer toward his own need to be examined by God:

> Search me, O God, and know my heart;
>   test me and know my thoughts.
> See if there is any wicked way in me,
>   and lead me in the way everlasting.
> (Ps 139:23–24 NRSV)

God, I hate your enemies! *Make sure, God, that I'm not one of them.* I wish you would just wipe out those who are wicked! *Is there some part of me that fits that bill? Search me out, God, and make sure that isn't the case.*

* * *

We are in Lent, which is a season of penitence. It is a season for diligently searching out the ways in which we are still living out the unredeemed life, the life of the old person that we sentenced to death in our baptism but that seems to keep getting stays of final execution. It is a season for repenting of *our* failure to allow God to decisively slay the wicked person that *we* once were. One of the spiritual disciplines that the church has valued and nurtured throughout the centuries, particularly during penitential seasons such as Lent, is the discipline of self-examination. The psalmist reminds us, however, that effective self-examination is not something that *I* do on my own, but something that God guides. It is God who brings to light what lurks in the shadows within us and still exerts control over us from those shadows.

It is God who shows us where and how to let more of that old person die so that more of the new person can come alive.

God is not afraid of the dark places in our hearts and minds, whether that darkness is the result of other people's injuries against us, of our own making, or—as is so often the case—some mixture of the two. That's because light *always* overcomes darkness. The sky's blackness does not darken the moon; a room's shadows never make a candle or a night-light dimmer. Light chases away darkness, never the reverse. Because of this, we don't have to be afraid of the truth about ourselves either, for whatever God brings to light, he does only to increase the domain of God's light within us, not to condemn us or shame us.

If we invite God to search us and to see if there be any wicked way in us, it's important that we resist the urge to jump in as defense attorneys for those parts of us that God's Spirit convicts. If we manage to defend what is dark in us against God's light, we haven't actually won anything. Indeed, this is an area in which lying to ourselves is a most self-destructive defense mechanism:

> If we say that we have fellowship with him while we're walking around in darkness, we're lying and not doing what is true. ... If we say that we haven't sinned, we're calling him a liar, and his word is not in us. (1 John 1:6)

We don't need to defend ourselves against the truth, for Jesus is already the advocate with the Father on behalf of that part of us that is most fully and eternally us. One essential facet of faith is to trust this: that Jesus is sufficiently for us that we can admit to, own, confess, and repent of all that we harbor within ourselves that is actually against us, against our becoming fully the Spirit-driven and Christlike person that God desires to make of us, against our becoming our truest selves in him.

The way of salvation is the way of siding with God against everything that is hostile to God's work within us of nurturing the fruit of the Spirit, of shaping and forming the new person that we are becoming in Christ, and that we hope fully to become even yet during this life. John Wesley strongly believed in the power of the Spirit finally to bring us to the point of allowing love for God and neighbor to drive us fully and without contradiction in all that we do. He called this "Christian perfection," but it's perhaps less daunting to think of it simply as letting in more and more of God's light until we have reserved no corner of ourselves for the darkness. Amen.

9

"How Far Is Enough?" (Palm Sunday)

Philippians 2:5–11

The week of Jesus' passion is also the week of the Jewish Passover, and the Passover has provided a frame of reference for the passion since the night *before* Jesus was given over to suffering and death, when Jesus took the bread and the cup at a Passover Seder with his disciples and gave them the shocking new meaning: "This is my body that is for you. ... this cup is the new covenant in my blood" (1 Cor 11:24-25).

A song that has been sung at Passover since at least the ninth century AD, but which arguably has much more ancient roots, celebrates God's generous kindness in rescuing Israel from Egypt by declaring that, had God only done a fraction of his works on Israel's behalf, it would have been enough. Had God stopped anywhere along the way, he would have given Israel cause enough to praise him and to acknowledge themselves to be forever indebted to God for his goodness toward them:

If God had brought us out from Egypt,
>   and had not rained down plagues upon them,
>   he would have done enough for us.

If God had rained down plagues upon them,
  and had not smitten their firstborn,
  he would have done enough for us.
If God had smitten their firstborn,
  and had not split the sea for us,
  he would have done enough for us.
If God had split the sea for us,
  and had not supplied our needs in the desert for
    forty years,
  he would have done enough for us.

And so the song proceeds through God's bringing his people to Sinai for the giving of the Torah, into the promised land, to Jerusalem, and to God's dwelling in their midst in the temple.

A similar sense of grateful awe seems to undergird the hymn to Christ that Paul either composes or recites in Philippians, as we are led to consider each step *further* that Christ took on our behalf in his incarnation and death. Indeed, I cannot help but hear the Passover song as a subtext for this early Christian hymn:

Had Christ given up his enjoyment of equality with
    God,
  and not humbled himself to take on human form,
  he would have done enough for us!
Had Christ humbled himself to take on human form,
  and not further abased himself to take on the form
    of a slave,
  he would have done enough for us!
Had Christ abased himself to take on the form of a
    slave,
  and not humbled himself further to become obedient to death,

> he would have done enough for us!
> Had Christ humbled himself to become obedient to
>   death,
>   and not submitted to death on a *cross*,
>   he would have done enough for us!

But at no point along the way did Christ say, "That's far enough to go for them."

*   *   *

Over the decades I have often heard preachers speak as if there were some great disconnect between Palm Sunday and Good Friday. How, they ask, did we move in the space of a single week from a triumphal entry into Jerusalem to the acclaim of thousands, waving their palm branches as symbols of the Messiah's coming victory and laying them in his path, to a gruesome flogging and crucifixion outside Jerusalem to the mock acclaim of Roman soldiers and of Jerusalem's leaders, waving their fingers as an expression of their victory over him? I would ask, How could the week have moved in any *other* direction? In an environment in which several would-be messiahs had already announced their candidacy and ended up routed by the Roman "peacekeeping" force, how could staging such an entry into Jerusalem at a major festival in obvious alignment with an ancient prophecy have *failed* to win for Jesus his own cross? Nothing speaks to me as loudly concerning Jesus' fixed intention to lay down his life—to be "obedient to the point of death, even death on a cross" (Phil 2:8)—as his staging of today's events. As we move through Holy Week, we may see Jesus wrestling with the consequences of what he has set in motion today as he prays in Gethsemane, "If this cup can pass from me," but we can be sure of this: what Jesus was looking for today was not really a parade into the city but a procession to Calvary.

The hymn in Philippians tells us something vitally important about Jesus' offering of himself on the cross. This is not merely an act by a human being, giving up his life to the God whom people had alienated by their disobedience, to win pardon and reconciliation for them. It *is* that, of course. Obedience was precisely what we had *not* given God. Adam had also been made "in the image of God," but Adam had considered being equal with God indeed something to be seized. This was the very enticement to disobedience employed by the serpent: "Eat, and you shall be like gods yourselves" (Gen 3:5). In that archetypal act are reflected all of our sins, every decision we've made to put ourselves and our wishes for our lives ahead of God and God's vision for the same—the ongoing rebellion of created beings against the Creator's claims upon those he had brought into being in the first place. Jesus charted a different path, the path of saying at every step of the journey, "Not what I want, God, but what *you* want," the path not of securing his own enjoyment of this life but of using this life to achieve God's ends for it. In this way, Jesus' offering of "obedience to the point of death" could become an offering *for us*, because Jesus had given to God all the obedience that we had not given—and did it specifically *for our sake*.

But this is not merely the act of a human being for human beings. Paul's hymn also describes an act by a divine Being, giving up divine rights and prerogatives, giving up his exalted dignity, lowering himself to our level and even below our level—"taking the form of a slave"—so as to break up the shell about our hearts that had been hardened against him and against our fellow creatures, our fellow human beings. On the cross of Jesus we do not see a man giving himself up to a torturous death to win over an angry, bloodthirsty God; we see God giving himself up to win over ungrateful, self-absorbed human beings. We see indeed the horror of the toll our sins have taken, but we see God having taken on flesh specifically so that he could bear that cost for us *in* the flesh.

> Amazing Love! And can it be
> That Thou, my God, wouldst die for me?[1]

Paul, however, did not share this hymn with his converts in Philippi *just* to say something about Christ. He shared it primarily to say something about being followers of this Christ, introducing his hymn with these words: "Have this disposition among yourselves, which was also in Christ Jesus" (Phil 2:5). Jesus' willingness to lay aside his rights and prerogatives for the sake of accomplishing God's purposes; his willingness to go the full distance and not draw any lines in the sand; his emptying himself instead of becoming "full of himself"; his willingness to divest himself of *everything*, even every last shred of dignity and of life itself in order to obey God and advance God's desire to restore people—all of this reveals something of the mindset that must drive us who follow this Jesus, who are bound to give for Jesus as he gave for us, in whom Jesus must take shape, so as to restore in us the image of God.

Paul invokes the example of Jesus specifically to support the instructions he had just given on how to interact with one another within the Christian community he planted in Philippi:

> Don't entertain rivalry or conceitedness in yourselves, but in humility consider the others around you to surpass you in dignity, each one of you looking out not for your own interests but each for the other's interests. (Phil 2:3-4)

---

1. Charles Wesley, "And Can It Be That I Should Gain?"

While the Christian group in Philippi was one of the least troublesome for the apostle, they weren't without their issues. At the moment, two leading women in the church—Syntyche and Euodia—were digging in their heels over some disagreement that Paul was too wise to name and were drawing other members of the church into their rival camps. Paul simply says, "Stop it." As soon as you start treating the other Christian as if his or her interests don't matter, as if he or she is less worthy of a hearing or deserves less consideration than yourself, you've lost sight of the issue that's always going to be more important than the one over which you're fighting: Are we approaching the other person with the mind that was in Christ Jesus? Take a moment and think about a person in your congregation who's gotten in your way, opposed something you thought important, failed to value you enough, or done something that moved you to contempt. What would it look like to take Paul's instructions to heart in regard to that person? What would it look like to empty yourself—to stop being so full of yourself—and put yourself at God's disposal to serve God's interests for that person?

Every church, it seems, has its own special T-shirt that it gives out or sells to its members. One of the churches I had previously served had the number "1" on the back of every one of its T-shirts, the implication being: "Everyone is number one at Christ United Methodist Church." I think they were trying to get at what Paul was after here, but maybe not quite strongly enough. After all, many of us already think we're number one at our church. What Paul is trying to cultivate is more of an attitude that "everyone *else* is number one here at my church"; *I* am here to make sure the people around me don't miss out on what God has and wants for them. I need to put myself at God's disposal and at their disposal to facilitate their arriving at the fullness of life—both here and hereafter—that God desires for them. A church full of people who have adopted *that* mindset, the mind of Christ, would be a powerfully nurturing community indeed! Who in the midst of such a community could fail to meet head-on the challenges that life threw their way? Who would fail to persevere in faithfulness to Christ, supported so completely along the journey by the strangers who had become genuine brothers and sisters through their mutual investment in one another? And who would fail to be drawn to such a community, to sink roots into such a community?

*   *   *

How far should *we* go for one another here in this congregation when we find ourselves at odds with a sister or brother? How far should *we* go when we discover that there is a need in our midst that we might have the resources or energies to meet, if we go far enough? How far is *enough* for us to go for one another in the global body of Christ, to give ourselves and what is ours away to show love to and solidarity with our sisters and brothers who have been driven out of their lands or beaten down in their lands because they wanted to hold onto Christ? How far is *enough* for us in terms of realigning our lives so that we serve God's kingdom agenda more and more directly and more and more fully? Have we reached the point where we've said, "far enough"? Do we find *our* "far enough" too soon?

The mindset that we see driving Christ *this* week—the mindset that Paul captures so perfectly in the hymn he recites—in part may shame us, who are so full of ourselves and so bent on getting our way or being treated as we think that we deserve that we sacrifice harmony in the church or even break fellowship with someone in the church or with the church as a whole. In part, what we see driving Christ *this* week obligates us, who have benefited so greatly from Jesus' pouring out of himself for

others, to follow in his way, to learn from him to empty ourselves and seek the interests of one another, to learn from him
that only *all the way* is far enough.

Now, if the end of Christ's story had been that cross, none of
us would be here today talking about him and celebrating this
week. I think (or, at least, I sincerely hope) that it will not come
as a spoiler to anyone here that the end of Christ's story is something quite glorious—all the more as it actually has no ending:

> Because of this, God also greatly exalted him
> > and favored him with the name that is above every
> > > name,
> in order that, at Jesus' name, every knee should bow—
> > that of every heavenly and earthly and under-
> > > worldly being—
> and every tongue should confess, to the glorification of
> > God the Father,
> > > that Jesus Christ is Lord. (Phil 2:9-11)

The language deliberately echoes God's own vow in Isaiah: "By
myself I have sworn: ... To me every knee shall bow, every
tongue shall swear allegiance" (Isa 45:23 ESV). No reader of Isaiah
would miss the implications of Paul's hymn about Christ: God
has invested the one who humbled himself to become human,
to take on a slave's role, to remain obedient even to the point
of the humiliating death of crucifixion—God has invested *this*
one with the honor of deity. The degradation of the cross was
not to be feared. God had Jesus' exaltation well in hand—not
merely the vindication of the abused honor of the Son of God
but the glorification of the human being that the Son of God had
become. Therein lies the great exchange—Deity allowed itself
to be brought down to the depths so that redeemed humanity
could be exalted to the heights with him.

Paul offers the end of Christ's story as assurance about the end of our story if we follow in his way. The way of setting ourselves aside and giving ourselves over to others—the way of the cross—is, in fact, the way toward exaltation before God. This counterintuitive claim is rooted in Jesus' similarly challenging saying, the truth of which is demonstrated most dramatically in Jesus' own story: "If anyone wants to make his life secure, he'll lose it; but if anyone gives his life away for my sake and for the sake of the good news, *that* person will make his life secure" (Mark 8:35). As we walk with Jesus through this, the climactic stage of his journey to "far enough," I pray that God's vindication of Jesus in the resurrection will awaken in all of us a firmer faith so as to follow Jesus far enough.

10

"A New Commandment" (Maundy Thursday)

John 13:1–17, 31–35

*I*t's impossible for them to have missed it. The large basin, the pitcher full of water, and the towel had all been sitting there in the room before Jesus and his disciples arrived at the house. As they entered the house, they all had to walk right on by this standard apparatus. Jesus might even have been watching the faces of his disciples as they noticed the vessels, looked around for a servant, gave the slightest shrug, and moved past to take their places on the cushions that had been arranged around the tables. *No servant in this house? No rinsing of the sand and dust from our feet? Oh, well. I wonder what's for dinner.*

Then, after everyone had selected their spot at the tables and settled onto the cushions, he does the unthinkable. I can almost hear Peter thinking to himself: "Why does he have to go and do that! This is so embarrassing! Why didn't one of the guys think to do this, so he wouldn't get up and put us through what he's about to do?" He looks over to James and John and shakes his head in disbelief, as if to say: "What do we keep the other nine around for, anyway?"

In the other three Gospel narratives of what went on in the upper room on the night before Jesus' death, the evangelists don't give any account of Jesus washing his disciples' feet. But they don't ignore the point of the lesson, either. In Luke's narrative of the course of this evening, we see a dispute arising among the disciples concerning which one of them had the highest standing among the group. Jesus won't allow *that* elephant to enter the room, let alone settle in unchallenged, so he says:

> Gentile rulers lord it over their subjects and those who hold authority among them are called "Benefactors," but *you're* not going to be like that. No, but let the one who has the greater dignity become as the junior member, and the leader as the one who does the serving. For who has the greater dignity? The one who reclines at the table, or the one who stands to serve? Everyone would say it's the one who reclines at the table, no? And yet *I* stand among you as the one who does the serving. (Luke 22:25–27)

On the night before his suffering and death, it seems to have been most on Jesus' mind to impress upon his followers once and for all this overturning, this shaking up, of worldly notions of status, social hierarchy, and the implications of the same for how we're going to behave toward each other and where we're going to draw the line between what we're willing to do and what we're not going to do. John's Gospel, as is so often the case, puts some real flesh on that word ("I stand among you as the one who does the serving") by showing us Jesus getting up from the couch and washing his disciples' feet.

* * *

Providing water and a basin for rinsing away the gritty dirt from sandal-clad feet appears to have been a widespread ritual of hospitality in the ancient Mediterranean. In well-to-do homes, household slaves would perform the task for the free-born members of the household and their guests. It could also be performed by any socially subordinate member of a household for those above them in the hierarchy of the home—in the Greco-Roman world, wives for their husbands or children for their parents. Disciples might perform such services for their rabbis as signs of respect. What one does not see, however, is social superiors performing this service for social subordinates. In the highly status-conscious world of the ancient Mediterranean, such lines were not crossed or confused.

So Peter's incredulous question—"Lord, are *you* going to wash *my* feet?"—followed by his strenuous objection—"There's no way that *you're* going to wash *my* feet!"—is imminently understandable, not only on the basis of Peter's regard for Jesus' dignity, but on the basis of Peter's regard for his own personal comfort. Such a status reversal was bound to be a dreadful embarrassment also to the *inferior* party. Jesus, however, can't let Peter off this particular hook: "Unless I wash you, you have no share with me" (John 13:8b). With characteristic drama, Peter responds, "Well, if it's really necessary, let's go all the way! Wash my hands and my head as well!" Jesus must have rolled his eyes (on the inside at least) as he patiently countered, "I don't have to wash every part of you, Peter, but you *do* have to let me do *this*."

Why did Jesus make such an issue of this with Peter? I do not think it was because there was something mystical in the act itself, as if this was some necessary purification, a kind of special baptism. But there was something mystical in each disciple allowing Jesus, the master, to perform this inappropriately humbling, status-smashing act of service. To be thus served by Jesus changes the one who has received the service. The one who has felt himself or herself thus served by Jesus will not shy, will not wince, at serving another.

After Jesus finishes making the rounds of the disciples' feet sticking out from their couches, he puts on his outer cloak again and asks the disciples, "Do you know what I have done to you?" (John 13:12 NRSV). ("Yes, Jesus," Peter thinks to himself, "you've made this evening extremely awkward, *thank* you very much.") The way Jesus' question ends is ambiguous in the Greek: it could be heard as "Do you know what I have done *for* you?" or "Do you know what I have done *to* you?" The NRSV chooses the latter, probably with very good reason. Jesus has not just done something *for* the Twelve, performing a service *for* them; he's done something *to* the Twelve. He's laid a challenge, an obligation upon them. It's a straightforward argument from the greater to the lesser:

> You call out to me, "Teacher" and "Lord," and you're right to do so, because that's what I am. If, then, *I*—your Lord and teacher—washed *your* feet, you also are obliged to wash one another's feet. (John 13:13-14)

If *I* can do it, *you* surely can do it. If *I* can set status and propriety as this world reckons them aside, *you* surely can set your narrower distances in status between each other aside and get down to the business of serving one another. In this paragraph we find something that is rare indeed in the Fourth Gospel—a saying of Jesus that we also find in one of the first three Gospels: "A slave does not have greater dignity than his master, nor does the person who gets sent on a mission have greater dignity than the one who sent him out on a mission" (John 13:16; compare Matt 10:24). In Matthew's Gospel, this saying braces the disciples to face hostility and persecution: if it happened to *me*, says Jesus, it will happen to *you*. In John's Gospel, this saying lays the obligation of mutual servanthood on all who claim Jesus as their teacher and their Lord. If this isn't beneath *me*, it's not beneath *you*. If you've experienced my washing your feet, Peter, if you've experienced how no act of loving service is beneath *me*, your master and Lord, you'll know that no act of loving service is beneath *you*, my disciple and follower. And if you know this, blessed are you if you actually go about putting this into practice henceforth (John 13:17).

Let me draw a modern analogy. Dishes had been piling up in the sink in the executive lounge. A number of the management team had already had to start putting their own dishes off to the side of the sink for lack of room in the sink. There was even some chatter about looking into the janitorial staff's performance, since they seem to have been slacking off. The CEO came in to get some coffee, noticed the dishes piling up, and heard some of the chatter. He took off his suit jacket, rolled up his sleeves, grabbed the sponge and soap and started doing the dishes and setting them in the empty drying rack. Then he went around the room, gathered any plates and cups that his management team had finished with, took those over to the sink, and washed them. He rolled down his sleeves, put on his jacket, got his coffee, and walked out. The CEO did something *for* his managerial staff, but he also did something *to* them. They all realized that any one of them could also take off his or her jacket, roll up his or her sleeves, and wash dishes—and now they had no excuse not to do so.

* * *

It's easy to apply this lesson to our life together as a church. If you see something not done that someone else ought to have attended to, especially if you think it's below you, remember what Jesus did on the night before his death. If the garbage needs emptying, if the sanctuary needs some picking up, if there are crumbs left scattered on a table in the library; if the visitation team isn't getting out to everyone you think they ought to be seeing, if the trustees aren't getting everything fixed in good time, if the rest of the parishioners aren't inviting enough people to our services ... you get the idea. In many churches, there are a lot of people with servants' hearts; in many churches, there are a number of people who, well, could probably pick up a basin and a towel a bit more frequently.

But, of course, Jesus' object lesson goes well beyond such trifling matters, just as Jesus' washing of the disciples' feet is a symbolic act that interprets the greater act of service on the part of the Suffering Servant—not merely laying down his garment and taking up a towel, but his laying down his life and taking up the cross. Indeed, at least one disciple clearly heard Jesus also saying, "If laying down my life for you is not beneath *me*, laying down your lives for one another in my family is not beneath *you*." This brings us to the episode that gives this evening its name: Maundy Thursday, "Maundy" being a corruption of the Latin *mandatum*, "commandment." On this evening before he gives up his life for all who would ever become his disciples, Jesus gives a new commandment: "Keep loving one another" (John 13:34).

In a sense, this is an old commandment, as the author of 1 John seems to recognize (2:7–8). We are familiar with the commandment given to Israel at Sinai, found in Leviticus 19:18—"Love your neighbor as yourself," adopted by Jesus as the companion to the greatest commandment, "Love the Lord your God with all your heart, all your mind, all your strength" (Deut 6:4; compare Mark 12:29–31). Jews continued to remind one another of this commandment, as for example in the Testaments of the Twelve Patriarchs, written not terribly long before Jesus' birth:

"Love your brothers and sisters, and put away hatred from your hearts, and love one another in action, in speech, and in your minds" (T. Gad 6.1); "Each one of you must love his or her brother or sister with a sincere heart" (T. Simeon 4.7).

In another sense, however, the commandment is new in one very significant way. As if Leviticus 19:18 did not lay enough upon us in terms of taking our neighbor into our circle of care, our scope of concern, now Jesus gives a new commandment that surpasses all that preceded: "Love one another just as I loved you" (John 13:34). Not merely, "Love your neighbor as yourself," but "Give yourself up to secure your neighbor's good." Taking up a towel for one another is an important first step; it's essential training in discipleship. But Jesus is calling us much further—to take up a cross for one another, to lay aside our own comfort, our own pursuits, our own delights, our own time and resources for the sake of meeting the very real needs of the sisters and brothers both in our midst and throughout the globe—to bestow on those most in need among Jesus' family the love and self-investment that Jesus bestowed on us.

* * *

John 3:16 is a verse that is often heard during Holy Week: "God so loved the world that he gave his only-begotten Son, that whosoever should trust in him might not perish but have eternal life." When planning music, I often have the choir sing a musical setting of this verse by John Stainer during Lent or Holy Week, an anthem that notably comes from the middle of his oratorio *The Crucifixion*. But we hear tonight about our necessary response to John 3:16, a connection also made explicit in 1 John 3:16, where John the elder appears to be commenting on the material we've heard tonight from the Fourth Gospel:

This is the message that you heard from the outset—
that we are to keep loving one another. ... We have
come to know love by this—that he laid down his life
on our behalf. So we ought also to lay down our lives
for our sisters and brothers. Whoever has this world's
goods and sees a sister or brother in need and with-
holds compassion from him or her—how does God's
love live in such a person? Little children, let's not go on
loving in word or in talk, but in action and in reality.
(1 John 3:11, 16–18)

Jesus asserts that *this* kind of loving service is what will show the
world that we follow Jesus; it will make the world recognize us
to be Christ-followers and, by implication, have to recognize
the reality of Christ even as the reality of effects demonstrate the
reality of the cause.

Christians were accused quite early on of turning the world
upside down (Acts 17:6). It is important that we continue in that
venerable tradition—of classifying no act of loving service as
below us but jumping up to be the first to stoop down, following
the example of our Lord and Teacher; of observing no hierarchy among ourselves that does not call the most ambitious to
the most humble service; of allowing Christ's love for us to continue to have force in this world by finding the ways in which we
are being called to lay our own lives down for one another in
love throughout the body of Christ. Amen.

11

"Living Like You'll Live Forever" (Easter)

Luke 24:1–12; 1 Corinthians 15:19–26, 51–58

*I*f it all seems a bit unbelievable, that's alright. The message of Easter—the news that Jesus had beaten death and walked out of the tomb—struck the people who had known Jesus and traveled with him for years as unbelievable as well. They had even heard him announce on several occasions that he was going to be crucified, buried, *and* raised to life again, and still, when the women returned from the empty tomb to report that two angels had appeared to them and said, "He's not in there anymore—he's on the loose in the world again," the eleven dismissed it as "an idle tale" and for the most part returned to their moping (Luke 24:11). They had seen what had happened to him—granted, from a safe distance. First, the thugs employed by the chief priests and then the thugs serving in the Roman peacekeeping force had made a complete mess of him. Then they nailed him up on a pair of planks between two other unfortunates and that was that. Game over. No bonus round.

It was difficult for the eleven to question what seemed—based on all observable evidence not only from that week but throughout their whole lives—to be the basic fact of life: death is the end. Alright, so maybe Jesus gave a *few* people a "bonus round," like that widow's son in the village of Nain, or that daughter of Jairus, the synagogue leader, or Jesus' own friend Lazarus, which was all pretty impressive, but all of them were just going to die again anyway. Jesus could sneak a little extra time for some people, but there's no beating death in the end.

It wasn't long at all, however, before the disciples were confronted personally with the risen Christ. He didn't quite look like himself—at least, a pair of disciples didn't recognize him as they walked for perhaps seven miles together from Jerusalem to Emmaus, until he broke bread at a table with them. In John's Gospel we find Mary Magdalene by the empty tomb mistaking Jesus for the gardener, until Jesus calls her by name. When he showed up in the midst of the eleven and their companions (in John's Gospel, he appears among them in the middle of a locked room), the disciples weren't sure if he was real or a ghost, until he told them to poke him and give him some food. It took a while for it all to sink in. It must have been so hard to believe, after seeing the triumph of death all around them for all their lives, that they knew someone who really *had* defeated death, who now lived a life in a body over which death had no more power. They *still* took another fifty days to process all this before they started preaching—and living—the implications of it all.

*   *   *

The apostle Paul, who also had the benefit of getting turned around by an encounter with the risen, glorified Christ, knew a great deal about living the implications of it all. Indeed, if he was going to prove faithful to God's commission to him to proclaim Jesus as the risen Lord, he would *have* to be willing to live the implications of following a resurrected Lord, which simply meant living *now* as if he was going to live forever.

I typically hear the expression "living like you're going to live forever" applied to people doing stupid things—like taking unnecessary risks for the thrill of it, putting a great deal of energy into work while allowing relationships with spouses or children to suffer for lack of investment, or just plain wasting precious time that one will never get back but some day will desperately wish one *could* get back. Living mindful of the fact that we *will* die one day *can* be a path to living wisely during the span of this mortal life. It *can* help us reflect on how to make the most of any given day in terms of pursuing what gives greatest value to our lives rather than allowing ourselves just to kill time in a kind of prolonged suicide. It *can* help us prioritize wisely, which usually means prioritizing people. (I wouldn't take back a single hour that I have spent playing with our boys, for example.) It can even help us stop investing ourselves in conflicts and concerns over the little things because we know that pouring any more of our limited time into such matters is just sending good money after bad.

More often, however, it seems that living mindful of the fact that we will, one day, die leaves us vulnerable to living in a selfish, even cowardly, manner. We find ourselves thinking more of what we are getting out of life and making sure that we get what we want out of life, even if that means giving up on a spouse who no longer makes us happy; even if that means spending 97 percent of our after-tax income on preserving the lifestyle to which we've become accustomed; even if that means getting behind public policies that hurt other people but are all right because they protect *our* interests. We are no longer motivated by virtue. The good of the other, whom we are to love as we love ourselves, is no longer the primary guiding value. Instead, we are seduced into an ethic of satisfying our own desires to the point that we are willing not only to withhold help from but to cause harm to others to do it. This is how death makes us its slaves. This is how death asserts its control, its power over us. This is precisely that from which Jesus died and rose again to free us.

If we are going to follow Jesus all the way, we need to discover an Easter faith. We need to understand that death is not the wall into which we slam at the end of our lives; death is not a mirror that should keep us looking only to *this* life and looking out to get all we can out of *this* life. Death is a door—one that Jesus has knocked off its hinges. We need to hear Jesus this morning, standing outside his tomb with the round stone rolled back again, saying: "I died, and look! I'm alive now for all ages to come—and I hold the keys of Death and Hades" (Rev 1:18). Only if we hear him say this and trust him that he can and will unlock *our* tombs will we be able to follow him when obedience, when gratitude, becomes costly. Only then will we trust him enough to give away our lives for his sake and for the sake of the gospel, believing his word that it is only *such* people who will ultimately make their lives secure.

* * *

Paul understood all of this very well. What we do not see in Paul is an attempt to have things both ways—a secure, comfortable life now and just enough of Jesus to have some insurance in case there's something after death. What we see instead is a complete reordering of life with a view to fulfilling the call that Paul understood God to have placed on his life—to announce God's Son throughout the nations that made up the Roman Empire (Gal 1:15-16). He took up an essentially itinerant life; a hard trade that required, however, only a few tools that could easily be carried as he moved from city to city; and hostility from everyone who felt threatened or betrayed by his proclamation of a crucified blasphemer as the Messiah of Israel, who loved gentiles every bit as much as Jews and would soon return to upset the entire Roman order.

Paul provides this summary of the downside of his life as a missionary and church planter:

> Five times I have received from the Jews the forty lashes minus one. Three times I was beaten with rods. Once I received a stoning. Three times I was shipwrecked; for a night and a day I was adrift at sea; on frequent journeys, in danger from rivers, danger from bandits, danger from my own people, danger from Gentiles, danger in the city, danger in the wilderness, danger at sea, danger from false brothers and sisters; in toil and hardship, through many a sleepless night, hungry and thirsty, often without food, cold and naked. And, besides other things, I am under daily pressure because of my anxiety for all the churches.
> (2 Cor 11:24-28 NRSV)

And all of that happened to him before the really bad stuff—his four years of imprisonment in Caesarea and Rome and his eventual execution under Nero. He can truly say: "If we've hoped in Christ only for *this* life, we're of all people the most wretched" (1 Cor 15:19). If there's no resurrection from the dead for *me*, why have I been doing all this? As Paul says just a few breaths later,

> Why do we put ourselves in harm's way every hour? It's like I'm dying out there every day! If I faced down people in Ephesus who were like wild animals, what did I gain from it? If the dead aren't raised—if *this* life is all there is—then let's eat and drink, for tomorrow we die.
> (1 Cor 15:30-32)

To what extent do we spend *our* lives hedging our bets? To what extent do we insulate ourselves from the possibility of ending up like Paul—the losers both here and hereafter because we failed to get all we could out of this life in the hope that Easter faith was real, perhaps to find out in the end that it wasn't real. This is, however, precisely the posture against which Jesus warned: "Those who seek to make their lives secure will lose them; those who spend their lives for my sake and for the sake of the good news will secure them" (Matt 16:25).

*   *   *

Paul understood that one had to go "all in," to live now like people who were assured of living forever and not hedge one's bets. Pastor Stephen Abur of Darfur, Sudan, understood this as well. He continued his work of preaching Christ in open-air evangelism and building up a congregation of believers there despite having received multiple death threats from Muslim zealots, who were enraged that former Muslims were embracing Christianity. Enough Sudanese Christian leaders had turned up dead for Stephen and his family to treat the threats as credible, yet they persisted in their witness and in their work. In the still-dark hours of the morning of March 2, 2018, Stephen, his wife, and their two daughters were found butchered (the reports say "like cows") in their house, after their attackers had set fire to the church building in which over a hundred converts, who had been disowned by their own families, were living.[1]

Theirs was an Easter faith. They continued to live as people who would live forever—for whom death might hold some apprehension, but not fear, such as might intimidate them into silencing their obedient witness to the Lord who loved them and gave himself for them. As I hear more and more such stories of

1. "Sudanese church pastor murdered with family for preaching the Gospel," Barnabas Fund, accessed July 13, 2018, barnabasfund.org/en/news/sudanese -church-pastor-murdered-with-family-for-preaching-the-gospel.

our sisters and brothers around the globe, I think more and more that our best response is not, "Well, I'm certainly glad that we live here where that sort of thing doesn't happen," or "Thank God we don't have to face anything like that." I don't think anymore that God calls for that degree of Easter faith from one family or person and calls for much less Easter faith from another family or person. No, I have begun to hear this: "If they faced *death* with that kind of an Easter faith, how should we live *life* with an Easter faith to match?" If they were willing to give their all on this side of death to continue the witness and work of Christ, sure that their Lord held the keys and would unlock death for them, putting their all into advancing their Lord's interests in Darfur, what would it look like for us to give our all on this side of death to advance our Lord's interests both here and throughout the world? Should I feel lucky that my faith journey doesn't require such sacrifice as is required of others and go back to enjoying my normal American life with all of its trappings? Or should I start reorganizing my normal American life more radically so that, maybe, my *living* will bear the same kind of witness to an Easter faith as the Abur family bore in their *dying*? The essential question that Easter places before us is this: Will we go on living for the sake of the enjoyment of *this* life, witnessing to the power of death, or will we live like people who are going to live forever, proclaiming by our selfless actions and courageous witness, "Death, where is your sting? Death, where is your victory?" (1 Cor 15:54b).

The good news of Easter is not merely that Jesus' story has a happy ending. It's the assurance that Jesus' resurrection is the first of many: "Christ has been raised from the dead, the *first fruits* from among those that sleep" (1 Cor 15:20). Where there are first fruits, the full harvest is not far behind. Christ's resurrection turned the tomb into a womb. It may swell now as its burden grows with each new death, but at the time of deliverance new life will burst forth as the dead are brought forth by God to live anew (Rev 20:13). The chief point of 1 Corinthians 15 is that you can't believe in the resurrection of Jesus without also believing in your own. And when you truly believe in your own resurrection, you will be free to give yourselves away for the good of others like people who have an endless supply of life—for you know that you really *are* going to live forever.

12

"Our Great High Priest" (Ascension)

Acts 1:1–12; Hebrews 9:11–14, 24–28

I have come across the term "story arc" more and more as television shows have become more complex. The increased use of such language reflects the increasing sophistication of some shows, where there are plots that are laid and find resolution within a single episode, but there are also plots that are laid in season 1 and continue to develop through many episodes, going through their own twists and complications until several seasons later. Today, we focus on a critical episode in Jesus' story arc—an episode that is in many ways a satisfying conclusion to his story.

If we were to read the Gospels of Luke or Matthew, we would begin with the birth of a child who is somehow not merely of this world but has come into this world from the divine realm. If we were to read John's Gospel, this is laid out all the more clearly: the Son of God, the eternal Word, descends into our world and into our story to accomplish a grand mission. We follow the complications of the conflicts that arise as he pursues this mission, with his adversaries ironically facilitating the Son's accomplishment of his ultimate goal for his mission—namely, his offering of himself upon a cross and God's glorious vindication in his resurrection. On this Ascension Sunday, we celebrate his return to the divine realm, in a kind of aftermath of the "real" action of his story.

This is precisely the way that Luke ends his Gospel, a nice season 1 finale: "Jesus led them out as far as Bethany and, raising his hands, he blessed them. And while he was blessing them, he departed from them and was borne aloft into heaven. And as they were worshiping him, they returned to Jerusalem with great joy, and they continued to bless God in the temple" (Luke 24:50–53). Cue end title music and credits.

Acts is the sequel to Luke's Gospel. It's the second season, as it were. And it opens in what has become a time-honored way for a second season to open—by stepping back and replaying the season 1 finale but this time with an important twist. The disciples are left as we were at the end of the first season, staring up into heaven with a sense that Jesus' story arc is completed with his return whence he came, his ascension back to the realm of God whence he descended. One can almost hear their thoughts: "We're sure going to miss him. It was great having him around, even if that resurrection body was a little spooky—with him just disappearing on us in Emmaus or his just showing up inside our room with its doors still bolted." We watch them gazing into heaven and we wonder: Is this the end of Jesus' story arc? Has our favorite character been cut from the show? An angel appears and announces, "No!" The story goes on—not just the disciples' story as they return to the city to await the promised Holy Spirit but *Jesus'* story as well: "This same Jesus, who has been taken up from you into heaven, will come in the same way as you saw him go into heaven" (Acts 1:11).

The ascension is the event that inaugurates a second story arc for Jesus. The one who came down from heaven to take on our humanity has returned to heaven, still bearing our humanity; the one who ascended to heaven will return again at the unforgettable and not-to-be-missed series finale. The Letter to the Hebrews echoes this: "Christ, having been offered once for all in order to bear the sins of many, will appear a second time—not for sins but for the salvation of those who eagerly long for him" (9:28). Jesus' story isn't yet completed. And we are living as part of this second arc, which encompasses the whole life of the church.

* * *

"Ordinary Time" is that long, yawning stretch of the Christian year between Pentecost and Christ the King Sunday—which celebrates the consummated lordship of Christ over all things, when indeed at last "*every* knee shall bow and *every* tongue confess that Jesus Christ is Lord, and this to the glory of the Father" (Phil 2:10–11)—just before the next Advent. Ordinary Time is *our* time; it represents the long season of the church's activity and work in the world, performed nonetheless in connection with and directed by Christ, who is the Head of the body, the church.

But Jesus, once enthroned as Lord and Anointed One, also has a story arc throughout this long season (by which I mean these 1,985 or so years so far, not just June through November). Jesus' departure at the ascension turns out not to mean Jesus' absence from the life of his people on earth. He keeps showing up in the second season. Stephen, the first to die as a result of his witness to Jesus, glimpses Jesus in glory at God's right hand. The glorified Jesus intersects with and dramatically changes the story arc of Saul of Tarsus, turning him around from persecutor to preacher of the risen Lord. We see the glorified Jesus again alongside John the Seer on Patmos at the far end of the Christian canon, still speaking words of instruction and warning to his congregations.

It is, mysteriously, this very ascension, this very departure from his followers in terms of physical presence, that makes possible Jesus' availability to *all* his followers by means of the Holy Spirit—and thus makes possible Jesus' continuing presence in every episode of the church's story, for as many seasons as this run extends. At the outset of season 1, God the Son had willingly limited himself to a body—first to the physical body of his incarnation, then to the spiritual body of his resurrection. It was indeed essential for him to ascend, to "return to the Father" in the divine realm (compare John 16:7-11), if he was to transcend that bodily restriction. He accomplished this, as he had promised, in the sending of his Holy Spirit—the Spirit of God that is also the Spirit of his Son—upon his disciples in every age, connecting the Son as the Head to the ever-growing body of his followers, who are the means by which the Son enacts his reign during this long interim. Many of us, hopefully all of us, know from personal experience how Jesus can be present with us, even while physically absent. When we sing "What a Friend We Have in Jesus," we're not confessing an absent mediator, but one who is very much present to us as we sing, indeed, as we "carry everything to God in prayer" sheltered by our "precious Savior, still our refuge," day after day, year after year.

*   *   *

Some of the richest reflections within the New Testament on the significance of Jesus' ascension for us are to be found in the Letter to the Hebrews. We have to reckon here with a basic fact: Jesus and his activities ceased to be observable to eyewitnesses when that cloud removed the ascending Lord from his disciples' sight. How is it, then, that the author of Hebrews goes on to speak of what Jesus did after he "crossed through the heavens" to enter "heaven itself," the eternal realm of God's dwelling? The answer is to be found in his reading of the Old Testament. As for so many early Christian teachers reflecting on the significance of Jesus and his work, so for the author of Hebrews the Old Testament provides the map for the journey that Christ ultimately undertakes. It stood to reason for them that, since those ancient oracles of God lined up so well in hindsight with what they could see in his ministry, his miracles, his suffering, his death, and his resurrection from the dead, they would also line up well with those parts of Jesus' story that they could not see (such as the Son's activity *prior* to his incarnation or his activity beyond his ascension) or did not *yet* see (such as his return to judge the living and the dead).

The author of Hebrews looks particularly to Leviticus 16 for one particular map that illumines Jesus' journey—both his journey outside the city to the cross and his journey into heaven itself. Leviticus 16 outlines the ritual for the Day of Atonement, the solemn offerings that Israel's high priest would undertake once per year in order to cleanse the people and the holy of holies from the accumulated pollution of a year's worth of sin. The relevant parts here center on the fate of the two goats that were involved in the ritual. The first goat, over whose head the high priest would recite, and thereby transfer, the sins of the whole people, would be sent outside the camp and into the desert, removing the people's sins from them. The second goat would be slaughtered, and the high priest would take a basin of its blood into the holy of holies—the innermost chamber of the temple, where the presence of God burned brightest—to cleanse it of the defilement caused by the people's sin, removing the memory of their sins from God's presence in the temple.

The author of Hebrews presents Jesus as our great high priest. He is the priest of whom all the priests of the line of Aaron were but prototypes. Jesus' death and ascension effected a cosmic Day of Atonement rite, universal in terms of scope, definitive in terms of accomplishment, in contrast to the sacrifices ongoingly and endlessly performed under the old covenant. He was a high priest who offered *himself*, going willingly outside the gate of the city—outside the camp—"in order to sanctify the people by means of his own blood" (Heb 13:12). He was the high priest who brought the evidence of his own death into the very presence of God to cleanse God's memory and God's presence of the defilement our sins produced:

> Christ, having become a high priest of the good things that were coming about, entered once for all through the better and more perfect tabernacle that was not made with hands (that is, not in this realm of created things) into the Holy Places, having established eternal redemption—and this not with the blood of bulls and goats, but with his own blood. ... Christ didn't enter into hand-crafted holy spaces, which were merely the model of the genuine ones, but into heaven itself, now to appear before God's presence on our behalf. (Heb 9:11–12, 24)

Having completed this universal and decisive priestly act, Jesus sat down at the right hand of God—an event not seen by the author but discerned from the map of Psalm 110, a text to which Jesus himself drew attention during his ministry as relevant to his story: "The LORD said to my Lord, 'Sit at my right hand until I make your enemies a footstool under your feet' " (Ps 110:1; Mark 12:35–36).

We must not imagine the author to be expressing the view that Jesus is merely sitting on his resurrected posterior for eternity. Rather, this is an expression of the completion and the completeness of his one great high priestly act of atonement:

> Every priest [on earth] must remain standing about, performing the daily religious service and offering again and again the same sacrifices that aren't able to take away sins, but *this* one, after offering a *single* sacrifice for sins, sat down at God's right hand. ... For by a single offering he has decisively perfected those who are being cleansed. (Heb 10:11–12, 14)

It is also an expression of his nearness to the God with whom he continues to intercede on our behalf, his very proximity assuring us that God will always receive us favorably, since our great high priest is right there at God's side. (This does not mean, of course, that he will always grant the particular help we request, but it does mean that he will always help.)

*   *   *

Jesus' sitting at God's right hand is also an expression of his reigning *now*, his participation in *God's* reign over the cosmos as a whole and over the earth and its people in particular. He is seated beside God "waiting until his enemies shall be set as a footstool under his feet" (Heb 10:13; Ps 110:1), and his call goes out now to all people to live in willing submission to his reign *now*, rather than in unwilling subjection to his reign (or worse) at his coming again. The events of ascension and Pentecost look forward to the texts and themes of Christ the King Sunday. Christ's reign is real and visible in the world to the extent that it is real and visible in our own obedience to his commands as the guiding force in our lives. Christ's lordship is only real for *us* to the same extent.

Jesus' ascension has ultimate implications for our story arc as well, as the author of Hebrews makes clear at several points. Jesus has entered into heaven itself as a forerunner for us (Heb 6:19-20); the Son who has entered into glory is also "leading many sons and daughters to glory" (Heb 2:10). An ancient prayer of the church makes this petition: "Mercifully grant that we, walking in the way of the cross, may find it none other than the way of life and peace."[1] The ascension of Jesus provides firm assurance and even strong incentive to follow indeed in the way of the crucified Messiah who has now taken the place of highest honor in the cosmos.

1. *The Book of Common Prayer and Administration of the Sacraments and Other Rites and Ceremonies of the Church together with The Psalter or Psalms of David According to the use of the Episcopal Church* (New York: The Church Hymnal Corporation, 1979), 220.

13

"Should We Let Him In?" (Pentecost)

Ephesians 3:14–21; John 16:7–15

The rhythms of church life—by which I mean the rhythms of church attendance and of our expenditures of energy at church—might suggest that Easter is the climax of the liturgical year, from which apex we ride a slow decline into the doldrums of summer. The climax of the liturgical year, however, is still ahead of us—even though there will be admittedly fewer of us here to experience it together. I'm speaking, of course, of Pentecost, the Sunday on which we celebrate the pouring out of the Holy Spirit upon the one-hundred-and-twenty or so disciples waiting together since the epoch-making weekend of Jesus' death and resurrection. That event is rightly celebrated as the birthday of the church.

It was *after* they were "clothed with power from on high" (Luke 24:49) that the disciples flooded the precincts of the temple to bear witness to all concerning the death and resurrection of Jesus and to call thousands to repentance and into the fellowship of Christ through the Holy Spirit in the very first day (Acts 2:41), "the Lord adding daily" thereafter "to the number who were being rescued" (v. 47).

I don't want Pentecost to take us by surprise this year, such that we aren't prepared to receive all that it holds for us. Jesus himself gave careful attention to preparing his disciples for their Pentecost. In our Gospel reading, we hear but one out of four references to this upcoming Pentecost within Jesus' Farewell Discourse, the Fourth Gospel's account of the instructions Jesus gave to his disciples on the evening before his passion and death. Jesus would continue to point them forward to Pentecost, moreover, in the period between his resurrection and his ascension, his physical departure from the visible realm.

* * *

On that night before his suffering and death—but also looking ahead to his returning to the Father at his ascension—Jesus assured his disciples: "I'm telling you the truth: it's to your advantage that I'm going away, because if I don't go away, the Advocate will not come to you. But if I go away, I'll send him to you" (John 16:7). I imagine that this was a tough sell. After all, it had to be fabulous to have Jesus *there*—to hear his teaching with the full conviction of the truth of his words that his presence (and the presence of God that it mediated) brought; to witness his miraculous healings and signs, the ocular proof of the power of God at work in him and, because in him, immediately available in their midst; to see and know personally, with the eyes of the body and not only the eyes of faith, him in whom they were placing such trust. Who has not wished to have been alive then, to have seen Jesus in action, to have met him in the body? Who has not considered Thomas ever so fortunate to have been able to put forth his hand, touch the wounds in the risen Lord's resurrected body, and know beyond the shadow of another doubt that he was risen, that everything he had said about himself proved true, that everything he taught was therefore reliable

as a bedrock foundation? I would gladly endure that mild slap
down—"Do you believe because you've seen me? Blessed are
those who believe without seeing!" (John 20:29)—to be able
to believe because I've seen. What could be better than having
Jesus *here*?

And yet, Jesus himself said to them—and all but told them
on oath by insisting, "I'm telling you the truth" (John 16:7)—that
things would be better for them, that they would gain greater
advantage, from his departure, because it would mean his sending "the Advocate." Had we started listening in to this discourse
from the beginning today, we would have heard him introduced
as "*another* Advocate" (John 14:16), one who would be even more
for them (and for us) than Jesus, the original Advocate, was for
them. This second Advocate is, of course, "the Holy Spirit, whom
the Father will send in my name" (14:26), says Jesus, "the Spirit
of truth, who proceeds from the Father" (15:26).

The question before us is: Are we experiencing this "better"
yet? Do we enjoy such a connection with the Holy Spirit, and
with the living Jesus through the Holy Spirit, that we are glad
no longer to have Jesus walking about the earthly sphere?

* * *

Paul certainly prayed that his converts in Ephesus—along with
new converts who would have joined the Christian movement
since his departure—would enjoy such a connection. In one
of those rare passages in which Paul opens up a window into
his own powerful prayer life, specifically how he prays for his
churches, we find him praying that they would enter into a rich
experience of God's Holy Spirit:

> I bend my knees toward the Father, from whom all father-
> hood in the heavens and upon the earth takes its name,

that he might grant you to be strengthened with power in your innermost self through his Holy Spirit, in accordance with his glorious bounty; that Christ might live in your hearts by faith while you sink deep roots and foundations into love, in order that you might have the power to understand and to fathom, along with all the saints, what is the breadth and length and height and depth of the unfathomable love of Christ; that you might be filled with *all* the fullness of God. (Eph 3:14–19)

Now, John Wesley was not a fan of what he called "enthusiasm," which he defined as "a religious madness arising from some falsely imagined influence or inspiration of God; at least, from … expecting something from God which ought not to be expected from him."[1] We, too, should want to be careful not to fall into the trap of imagining ourselves inspired by God when we are not, nor to fall into the trap of "expecting something from God which ought not to be expected from Him." But I think we should seek to be equally careful not to expect too little from God—not to be so wedded to a "reasonable religion" that we shut ourselves off from the intimate knowledge of God and the flooding of our lives and our congregations with the power of God that Paul, at least, seems to be convinced that God wishes to provide (unless Paul himself is praying in vain).

Paul's prayer for the Christians in Ephesus—and I might presume that he would have prayed it for us as well, had he any inkling we would be gathering in Jesus' name nearly two millennia later—was for an *experience*. It was for an *encounter* with divinity that would presumably have a starting point but not an ending point. It was for the invasion of our inmost selves

---

1. John Wesley, "The Nature of Enthusiasm," in *The Works of John Wesley*, vol. 5, 3rd ed. (London: Wesleyan Methodist Book Room, 1872), 470.

by God's Holy Spirit, an invasion that would flood us with both power and a Person—not power for us to do what we wish, but power that comes in the divine Person of God the Holy Spirit, accomplishing what *he* wishes in us, among us, and through us. The second petition seems to me to be a consequence of the fulfillment of the first—that Christ would live within each one of us and among all of us together, bringing with him an experience of divine love that, at one and the same time, is so great that it cannot be measured but is so full and real that we *feel* its limitlessness. The third petition is the most paradoxical—that the infinite and boundless God in all his fullness should somehow come to occupy this infinitesimal space of "me." How could that ever happen except by God's settling within us, filling us with God's Holy Spirit? If it sounds a lot like possession, I think we're on the right track.

Should we let him in?

He *will* mess with everything if we do. But what might we hold on to that would be of greater value to us, that would bring us greater joy and fullness, than to "fathom the unfathomable love of Christ," to know the indwelling power of the Holy Spirit in our inmost selves, to experience the fullness of God firsthand and thus to know that, having God, we have it all? I personally would think it a great tragedy for us to go through our whole lives enacting the forms of piety but remaining closed off from its power.

Should we let him in?

* * *

Let me tell you, briefly, a story of a church that did. The pastor—I should say "rector," as this was an Episcopal church—visited another Episcopal church that had let the Holy Spirit in and spent some time corresponding with its rector. After a time of study, he led his parish through a series of sermons exploring the scriptural witness to the Holy Spirit and the scriptural vision for Spirit-led lives and Spirit-led churches. At some point in this pilgrimage, they prayed, and the Spirit showed up. Most in the congregation were suffused with a new and deeper love for God, for one another, and for the people outside their walls. They began meeting together more often, informally and in newly formed small groups, praying with and for one another, calling down God's help, favor, guidance, and Spirit upon one another. They began worshiping with a new passion for God. The old Anglican hymns came alive as vehicles of praise, adoration, and prayer. As might be expected, new songs were brought into the repertoire as well, bringing an added dimension to worship. The old liturgy took on a new life—the words didn't change, but the people had changed. When the time for prayer came around, people were unafraid to pray out loud and to pray with confidence.

Some admittedly strange things started happening as well, though these had become quite routine by the time I became part of the congregation. In the Sunday morning service, or the Wednesday evening teaching service, or in small groups— always at the appointed time for such things—someone might say something that he or she believed had been given him or her from the Lord. Generally, these would be sifted and confirmed or discarded over the course of the week. Someone might start praying in a language that was not recognized—what is commonly called "speaking in tongues." Now, I have to admit that I had serious doubts about this phenomenon myself. I loved the people. I respected their ardor for God and for genuine discipleship, but this part seemed a bit much—until, that is, a retired elementary school math teacher started praying over me in Greek. I can still remember a line from her prayer: *chairein en tē aretē tou kyriou,* "that he might rejoice in the excellence of the Lord."[2]

But the most important thing about this influx of the Holy Spirit into the lives of individual disciples and into their corporate life together was the level of love for one another and for the stranger in their midst that this engendered. It was a church to which I was eager to invite people (as indeed, were many), because there was something there that was unmistakably beyond the everyday. It was a place where connection with God was palpable. Those whom I brought almost never failed to be impressed by the spirit of the congregation and by the experience. I hold in my mind Paul's own vision for Christian worship and the manifestation of the Holy Spirit in the midst of the assembly: "If all are speaking prophetic utterances in the Spirit and an unbeliever or outsider comes in, he is convicted by all, he is called to account by all; the hidden secrets of his heart are brought out into the open and in this way, falling on his face to worship God, he will announce, 'Truly God is in your midst'!" (1 Cor 14:24–25).

* * *

I would like for us to be that kind of church. I would never presume that there are only certain ways that the Holy Spirit will be revealed, but I *do* presume that the Spirit's presence is *unmistakable.* I'd like for the presence and power of God to be so real and palpable here—something that comes to pass because the Spirit of God is vitally present in us and manifest through us and among us—that the visitor goes away not merely thinking, "Wow, those were really welcoming people" (though I *do* want

2. The portion that I remember literally reads "to rejoice in the excellence of the Lord," but I knew that she was praying for *me.*

the visitor always to leave with that impression!), but rather, "God is truly in your midst!"

The season after Easter was, for the first disciples, a time of waiting and praying for this "power from on high," this anointing with the Holy Spirit that Jesus promised. As we approach Pentecost this year, I would like to invite you—as many of you as are attracted to the experience that Paul's prayer envisions, who want to find out what's better than having Jesus here in the flesh with us—to spend these next few weeks as did those first disciples. I want to invite us all to wait in our own metaphorical upper rooms with the expectancy of being clothed with power from on high. I want to invite you to pray to God about receiving more of God's Holy Spirit yourself and about releasing more of God's Spirit in our midst. This is a prayer that we can count on God answering—for, as Jesus is remembered in Luke's Gospel to have said, "If you, being wicked, know how to give good gifts to your children, how much more will your Father from heaven give the Holy Spirit to those who ask him?" (Luke 11:13).

Let's let him in.

14

"New Spirit, New Heart" (Pentecost)

Ezekiel 36:24–28; Romans 8:1–17

*E*zekiel understood that at the heart of Israel's problem was the problem of Israel's heart. Many in Israel had lost their heart for God and God's covenant. They had long since forgotten God's benefits in delivering them from slavery in Egypt, leading them to take possession of the land that he had promised to their ancestor Abraham, providing them with all that was needful for a good life enjoying God's gifts. They wanted to be like other nations, living under the protection and patronage of powerful kings like Saul and David, rejecting God as their sole protector and patron. They wanted more than the covenant-shaped life would allow them. They didn't want to leave the gleanings of their fields for the poor, preferring to keep every bit of their land's produce for themselves. They didn't want to restrain themselves from increasing their lands at their neighbors' expense. They didn't want to honor God and God's temple with their tithes and offerings, preferring to institute their own temples and cult shrines throughout the land and to worship however and whomever they saw fit. They didn't want to restrain their anger, their enmities, their grudges, their factions and power plays, their extramarital sexual cravings, or their greed as God's law required of them. Of course, there were always the faithful among the people, but the stink of the rebellion of the unfaithful among them had overpowered the pleasing odor of covenant faithfulness, and God was moving in to take out the trash.

God was simply proving faithful to his own covenant promises. God told Israel the good that he would continue to bring upon them if they honored him and his gifts by keeping the covenant with him and the devastation he would bring upon them if they dishonored him and his gifts by dishonoring their covenant obligations. The majority of the Old Testament prophets warned Israel of those consequences and urged them to return en masse to lining themselves up quickly with the covenant's requirements, but the people's collective heart had become stone as far as God and the covenant were concerned. And so devastation came upon the northern kingdom of Israel and its scattered inhabitants in 721 BC with the Assyrian conquest and upon the southern kingdom of Judah and its scattered inhabitants in 587 BC with the Babylonian conquest.

Ezekiel also knew, however, that God would not abandon his good purposes for God's people. If Israel had proven unfaithful to the covenant that had promised them life, surely God would take the additional step of changing them from the inside out so that they *could* prove faithful to the covenant and enjoy God's promised blessings. What Israel lacked the power to do, God would empower them to do. And so we hear these astounding promises spoken in God's name:

> I will take you from the nations, and gather you from all the countries, and bring you into your own land. I will sprinkle clean water upon you, and you shall be clean

> from all your uncleannesses, and from all your idols I will cleanse you. A new heart I will give you, and a new spirit I will put within you; and I will remove from your body the heart of stone and give you a heart of flesh. I will put my spirit within you, and make you follow my statutes and be careful to observe my ordinances. Then you shall live in the land that I gave to your ancestors; and you shall be my people, and I will be your God. (Ezek 36:24-28 NRSV)

Israel needed a radical change of heart; they needed a heart that would be tender and sensitive again to God, so as to care deeply about how they were relating to God, how they were walking before God, what their walking said about their love for God and devotion to their covenant with God. But, Ezekiel says, God knew that they needed even more. They needed for God's own Spirit to enter them, to live within them, to direct and empower their covenantal response to God: "I will put *my* Spirit within you." This is the "new Spirit" that makes possible a "new heart" as well as a new future with God, one in which Israel would experience the covenant's promised blessings on its collective obedience and not its promised curses on its collective disregard for God and God's righteousness.

*   *   *

Paul understood the problem quite similarly—save that, in the death and resurrection of Christ, God was expanding the scope of his concern and his covenant quite dramatically. As he would put it in Galatians:

> Christ redeemed us from the law's curse by becoming a curse on our behalf (as it is written, "Cursed is anyone left hanging on a tree"), in order that the blessing pronounced upon Abraham might come upon the Gentiles in

Christ Jesus—in order that we might receive the promised Spirit through faith! (Gal 3:13–14)

Paul believed that, in Christ, God was circling back at last beyond the covenant that he had made with Israel to the promise that he had made to Abraham: that *all* the nations would receive God's blessing through him and through his offspring—for Paul, the offspring par excellence, namely Christ Jesus. And Paul unambiguously declares this promised blessing to be the Spirit!

Paul's letter to the Christians in Rome serves as Paul's introduction of himself and his message to the churches in the capital city of the empire. Even though Paul knows a good number of Christians in Rome, he's not yet been to Rome himself, and the majority of Roman Christians have not made his acquaintance. Romans is a kind of stewardship sermon, for Paul wants the Roman Christians to support his ongoing mission to points west of Italy, specifically to Spain, now that he has made the rounds from Syria through Dalmatia in the eastern Mediterranean. Paul therefore wants to lay out his understanding of the good news quite carefully and fully so that the Roman Christians will have a chance to think about what they would be supporting should they partner with Paul.

Paul is particularly emphatic in this letter that the good news of Jesus calls people to a change of life. He's been misrepresented in some circles as preaching grace as an excuse for making continued room for sin in one's life (Rom 3:8; 6:1, 15); he wants to make it crystal clear that this is *not* the case. Just two chapters prior to our reading today, we find Paul making these declarations:

Are we to keep on sinning in order that grace may abound? Heck, no! We who *died* to sin—how will we keep *living* in it? Don't you know that as many of us as were baptized into Christ Jesus were submerged into his death? We were buried, then, with him through immersion into his death in order that, just as Christ was raised from among the dead through the Father's glory, so also we might walk in a new kind of life. (Rom 6:1-4)

So don't let sin continue to be the dominant power in your mortal body, to make you keep obeying your body's cravings, and don't keep offering your embodied life to sin as *its* tool for doing what is unrighteous. Instead, offer yourselves to God as people who have come alive again out from among the dead, and offer your life in the body to God as *his* tool for righteous action. (Rom 6:12-13)

The promise of the good news is that "the person you used to be was crucified in order that the body driven by sin might be set aside, in order that we should no longer live as sin's slaves" (Rom 6:6), that "sin will not be your boss, because you're not living under law but living under grace" (Rom 6:14).

This is a great promise, but I wonder to what extent we are experiencing the fulfillment of this promise in our lives. Are we living in the victory over sin and over the sub-Christian attitudes and actions it incites that Paul proclaims? Does sin continue to master us as it kicks up resentment, anger, and that sense of injured merit within us? As it prods us to any of a wide variety of self-centered indulgences by which we seek to distract ourselves from the emptiness of our souls? Do we find ourselves giving our embodied life over to acting out sin's impulses, allowing it to achieve its ends in our relationships and realities instead of giving ourselves over consistently to God for God to achieve his ends in and through us? I don't find myself consistently there, where Paul says Christ's death has the power to take me. Do we perhaps even find ourselves to be like stone where God's love and leading are concerned, with the person that we *used* to be still very much the person that we *remain*?

Paul was acutely aware not only of the promise of the good news but also of the problem of the human condition—the problem of knowing the right thing to do and failing to do it, of knowing the wrong thing to do and failing to resist doing it. As he writes in the paragraphs immediately preceding our reading today:

> The good to which I aspire, this I *don't* do; but the wickedness I *don't* desire deep down—*this* is what I end up doing! But if I am doing what I don't really want to be doing, it's no longer *me* who's doing it, but *sin*—that power that is living within me. (Rom 7:19–20; see also 7:15, 17)

Paul writes these paragraphs from the perspective of living under the covenant law, like those Israelites who failed to keep covenant with God prior to the devastations of the Northern and Southern Kingdoms—and like those Israelites who continued not to walk in the covenant, whose hearts became stone once again, leading to the ongoing experience of gentile domination and, eventually, to the second destruction of Jerusalem and its temple under Rome in AD 70. A great many Christians, however, can also relate to the impasse that Paul describes— knowing the righteousness that God desires to see in our lives and finding themselves far more inclined toward selfishness and sin. We've probably all been there at some point, perhaps at many points. What not enough Christians seem to realize is that God does not leave us in this miserable condition, powerless to attain our holiest aspirations and doomed ever to fall back under the power of sin.

If we find ourselves still exclaiming with Paul, "Wretched person that I am! Who will save me from this death-bound body" in which sin has such power? (Rom 7:24), we have not yet experienced all that Christ has made available for us. It's *that* which causes Paul immediately to exclaim, "But thanks be to God through Jesus Christ, our Lord!" (Rom 7:25) as he moves to God's solution for the problem of the human condition— namely, the provision of the Spirit:

> The law of the Spirit of life has set you free in Christ Jesus from the law of sin and death ... in order that the just requirement of the law might be fulfilled in us who live not in alignment with the flesh but in alignment with the Spirit. (Rom 8:2, 4)

The contrast is unmistakable. Before God's work within us, sin was the power living within us, possessing us, driving us. The promise of the good news, however, is that God sets a new power loose to live within us, to possess us, to drive us.

> Those who live in the domain of the "flesh" are unable to please God. But *you* are not living in the domain of the "flesh," but in the domain of the Spirit, since God's Spirit is living in you. ... If the Spirit of the One who raised Jesus from the dead lives in you, the One who raised Christ from the dead will also make your mortal bodies to live through his Spirit that is living in you. (Rom 8:8–9, 11)

Christ has given us two things that open up for us the promise of the good news. The first is his own death and resurrection—his death, not only as an act of supreme obedience that reconciles us to God and sets aside the record of our own disobedience but as an act that communicates spiritual power to us each and every day because of our baptism. The death and resurrection of Jesus holds ever before us the opportunity and the obligation to die with him to our old self with its cravings and to live a new life for God. It is *both* opportunity and obligation. It is *opportunity*, because only those who die to self and live for God will live forever, and Christ has opened up this possibility for us. It is *obligation*, because "he died for all in order that those who continued living might live no longer for themselves but for him who died and was raised on their behalf" (2 Cor 5:15). We owe it to him to fulfill in our own lives the purpose for which he laid down his own life for us. "We *are* debtors," Paul says in Romans 8:12, "but we don't owe the *flesh* anything more."

The second thing that opens up the promise for us is this marvelous gift of the Holy Spirit, God with us, God within us. The promise of the good news that Paul articulated in Romans 6 — "Sin will not be your boss, because you're not living under law but living under grace" (Rom 6:14) — is made reality as the Spirit of the living God, that supreme grace, that supreme *gift*, of God becomes the dominant and driving force in our lives. As Paul had put it earlier in his letter to his converts in Galatia, "Walk in line with the Spirit, and there's no way that you're going to bring to pass what the flesh craves" (Gal 5:16). The good news proclaims the unqualified promise of the Spirit's victory over sin in us, so that we may indeed live for God in the manner that pleases God.

We can't leave this passage only focusing on the power of the Spirit for a transformed life without also hearing Paul's word about the power of the Spirit for a transformed relationship with God:

As many as are led by God's Spirit, *these* people are God's sons and daughters. ... You received a Spirit of adoption,

in whom we call out "Abba, Father." The Spirit himself
bears witness alongside *our* spirit that we are God's children. (Rom 8:14–16)

It is the Holy Spirit who tells us who we are before God and who
God will be for us, and whose witness within us gives us assurance of our place in God's family and in God's love. It is the Holy
Spirit that brings home to us Jesus' words of assurance, "Don't
be afraid, little flock; it is your Father's good pleasure to give
you the kingdom" (Luke 12:32). It is the Holy Spirit who stirs up
within us the necessary trust in the Father to let go of the person
that we used to be, with all of his or her desires, demands, and
requirements, to become the person that God wishes to make of
us—the person in whom Christ has come fully alive.

*   *   *

Do you want to know God more intimately—not just as *the* Father
but as *your* Father? Do you desire to experience unequivocal
victory over sin and the ways in which your old, self-centered
person derails your highest aspirations for new life in Christ?
Are you ready to stop letting your expressions, words, and
actions contribute to the brokenness in the world because of
sin and selfishness and let all of your expressions, words, and
actions contribute to God's redemptive activity wherever you
find yourself? If you feel yourself inclining positively in these
directions, take heart—it's a sign that you indeed have a tender
heart toward God, not a heart of stone. Take heart also because
God richly provides his Holy Spirit to accomplish all these things
in you and through you. Paul assures us that we were sealed with
this Holy Spirit when we put our trust in Christ (Eph 1:13), but
in the same letter he urges us to "keep allowing yourselves to be
filled up with the Holy Spirit" (Eph 5:18), to earnestly seek that

the Holy Spirit should become the indwelling power within us, training ourselves to discern the Spirit's leading so that we can keep walking in step with the Spirit. If this seems beyond our reach, we simply need to trust God's promise the more: "I will put my Spirit within you" (Ezek 36:27).

15

"An Unfailing Endowment" (Pentecost)

Luke 24:44–49; 1 Corinthians 12:1–14

I recently spent some time trying to get a handle on all the financial resources at our church's disposal and on the church's financial strength and stability. What would you say if I were to tell you that, while doing some digging in our congregation's history, I discovered something remarkable—a bequest made by one of the founding members of this congregation to create an endowment for the church that had somehow not been properly recorded or filed, such that we had entirely forgotten about it. This endowment has been growing for almost forty years, and we've never drawn off the accumulated interest. As a result, it has grown so large that the annual interest it accrues now is sufficient to fund fully a third of our budget. This had escaped the notice of the Wills & Memorials Committee; it had escaped the notice of the treasurer; it had even escaped the notice of our Finance Committee Chair. (So now you know this is all a fiction, since *nothing* escapes the notice of our Finance Committee Chair!)

The authors of the New Testament teach us that we *do* have an unfailing endowment, one whose supply will always exceed our need. It is one that is sufficient to fuel all our ministries and, indeed, allow us to accomplish more than we can presently imagine—if the scriptural witness to this endowment is reliable in what it depicts. It is an endowment that I fear we do not draw upon enough as we seek to resource the work of God in our midst and in our world, and as we ourselves seek to facilitate that same work through our own participation in it.

I'm speaking, of course, of the Holy Spirit. In a previous sermon we thought together about what this endowment offers us in terms of our individual lives as we give ourselves more and more to the Spirit's leading rather than to the leading of those self-centered impulses within us that have not yet succumbed to that death with Christ that we embraced in our baptism. God endows us with his Spirit, however, not only for our transformation and the transformation of our relationships but also for our empowerment as the vehicles through which God accomplishes the transformation of this world.

*   *   *

In our reading from Luke's Gospel, we hear Jesus' final pronouncement to his disciples prior to his ascension: "I am sending upon you what my Father promised. As for you, stay put in the city until you have been endowed with power from on high" (Luke 24:49). Jesus speaks, of course, of the pouring out of the Holy Spirit on Pentecost, just ten days after his ascension, as Luke will recount in chapter 2 of his sequel, the Acts of the Apostles. In the first instance, the Holy Spirit brings empowerment for effective witness. The Spirit makes it possible, in Jesus' words, "that repentance and forgiveness of sins should be proclaimed in my name to all the nations, starting from Jerusalem" (Luke 24:47). This endowment provides Peter with the needed resources to deliver his inspired—his truly "in-Spirited"—Pentecost sermon, to which over three thousand Jewish pilgrims in Jerusalem responded positively (Acts 2:40-41).

Let us not forget the miracle of Pentecost, which preceded Peter's preaching and drew the attention of Jewish pilgrims from every corner of the known world—the proclamation of the mighty works of God by the disciples in a bewildering variety of languages native to every region of the eastern half of the Mediterranean basin. As we continue to read Acts itself and the rest of the New Testament, we find that Pentecost was not merely a one-off, standout event; it was the inauguration of a new era in which the Holy Spirit would be widely, stunningly, and unmistakably experienced in the community that formed around the confession of Jesus as Messiah and Lord and in which the Holy Spirit would regularly manifest his presence and power to and through that community.

*   *   *

Paul begins to treat the topic of spiritual gifts in our epistle reading (1 Cor 12:1-14), though he continues to develop this topic through 1 Corinthians 13 (the famous "love" chapter, which you can almost always hear read at Christian weddings) and 1 Corinthians 14.

> Now, brothers and sisters, I don't want to leave you in the dark concerning things spiritual. You know that when you were gentiles you were led about, wherever you were led, to idols that cannot speak. Therefore I make known to you that no one speaking by God's Spirit says, "Jesus be cursed," and no one is able to say, "Jesus is Lord" except by the Holy Spirit. (1 Cor 12:1-3)

While it is tempting to explore what on earth could have made it necessary for Paul to point out that "no one speaking by

God's Spirit says, 'Jesus be cursed,' " we need to remain focused on the principal topic here. These Christians in Corinth have spent their lives worshiping gods who don't speak to human beings (since, as Paul views them, they're not real at all), but now they're dealing with a God who *does* speak, and it is vitally important for them to learn how to listen to God—to learn to recognize when it is God's Spirit that is speaking versus when it is some *other* spirit or just some voice within themselves usurping divine authority to promote their own agendas. This requires some spiritual maturity and personal discipline, but the possibility of hearing God's voice so as to be able to respond with obedience makes any investment in growing in this area worthwhile.

Paul continues:

> Now there are different kinds of gifts, but the same Spirit, and different kinds of service, but the same Lord, and different kinds of exhibitions, but the same God working all these things in everyone. The manifestation of the Spirit is given to each person to bring about what is beneficial.
> (1 Cor 12:4–7)

Paul finds himself having to make a case in 1 Corinthians for the value of the whole spectrum of the Spirit's gifts and manifestations because the Christians in Corinth appear to be most enamored with the flashiest manifestation—speaking in tongues. They need to learn to value the more practical manifestations of the Spirit, those that actually help Christians serve one another and help Christians connect powerfully with non-Christians. Paul's point is that the same divine power—indeed, the same divine *Being*—stands behind and is present in each kind of manifestation, and that the same divine Being determines who will manifest what gift to what end. It's not about showing your own spiritual status or virtuosity; it's about opening yourself up to be moved and deployed by the Spirit for God's own purposes and for the good of others.

I've been a part of several churches that have had their parishioners fill out so-called spiritual gifts inventories, which are really inventories of our natural inclinations, interests, and abilities. These are not to be despised or overlooked, and they are indeed to be channeled toward the doing of what is pleasing in God's sight—toward what advances God's interests in our situation and in the world. However, they ought also not be confused with the ways in which we are endowed by the Spirit's working within us with gifts for the good of the whole body of Christ, often quite apart from our natural inclinations, interests, and abilities.

There's no danger, of course, confusing Paul's spiritual gifts inventory with natural endowments:

> To one person, a word of wisdom is given through the Spirit; to another person, a word of knowledge in accordance with the same Spirit; to another, faith by the same Spirit; to another, endowments of healing in the one Spirit; to another, demonstrations of power; to another, prophecy; to another, the ability to discern spirits; to another, various kinds of languages; to another, the interpretation of languages. One and the same Spirit works all these things, apportioning to each person just as the Spirit wishes. (1 Cor 12:8–11)

What strikes me as most remarkable about Paul's description of the ways in which God makes God's Holy Spirit known in the Christian assembly is how casual Paul is about it all, as if these manifestations are as regular in his experience as an opening song or hymn, a morning prayer, and an offering are for us! Paul creates different catalogs of the Spirit's endowments for the church elsewhere in his letters, so we shouldn't hear this list as comprehensive—but we should still hear this list, all the more as it can challenge our own experience of God's operation within Christian community and the degree to which we know ourselves to be acting in response to the Holy Spirit (that is, the degree to which we know the Holy Spirit to be prompting our actions).

It's important to notice up front that Paul defines these gifts not as powers that become the personal possession of the believer but as "manifestations of the Spirit" (1 Cor 12:7). They are gifts *for* the Christian assembly, *from* the Spirit, *through* a willing, obedient, Spirit-sensitive person. They convey no status on that person; they do not come about because that person wishes them to but because the Spirit has something for the occasion. Spiritual gifts are not about an increased ability to bring about what *I* want to see happen but about a greater availability to God to bring about what *God* wants to see happen.

The "word of wisdom," the "word of knowledge" (which may be what Paul will refer to in chapter 14 as a "revelation"), the "prophetic utterance"—by means of all of these the Spirit imparts a supernatural perception into a person's heart, into a situation, and into God's perspective on things. In chapter 14, Paul will speak of "the gift of prophecy" communicating a word from the Lord to the assembly for "edifying, encouraging, and consoling" (1 Cor 14:3-4). He will speak of the unbeliever walking into the Christian assembly where believers are exercising these gifts, with the result that "the secrets of his heart are brought out into the open," which sounds like "words of knowledge" to me, opening up the unbeliever to the presence and power of God and positioning him or her strongly for repentance and conversion (1 Cor 14:23-25).

Prophetic utterances were not uncommon. In Acts, we read of Agabus revealing to the Christians in Antioch that there would be a widespread famine, mobilizing proactive relief efforts for the more economically vulnerable Christians in Judea (Acts 11:27–30). Agabus returns later in the story, announcing to Paul that imprisonment would befall him in Jerusalem (Acts 21:10–12). In 1 Timothy we read about a prophetic utterance spoken over Timothy in connection with the laying on of hands (perhaps his commissioning for leadership in Ephesus?) and the imparting of some unspecified endowment of the Spirit (4:14). The second and third chapters of Revelation provide seven stellar examples of prophetic utterances as the author communicates the glorified Christ's assessment of the various congregations' strengths and weaknesses and calls them to courses of action that will bring them into alignment with him.

It is probably in connection with these manifestations that we should place the gift of "distinguishing between spirits"—recognizing whether it is indeed God or some other spirit or the speaker's own self behind the utterance (see also 1 Thess 5:19–21; 1 John 4:1–3). Paul also expects the Spirit to empower believers to speak in tongues, whether these are actual human languages, as happened at Pentecost, or other languages that may reflect "the languages of angels," to which Paul will refer at the outset of chapter 13 ("If I speak in the languages of human beings or of angels, but lack love ..."). Paul may downplay the value of this manifestation in 1 Corinthians largely because it is overplayed in Corinth, but his evaluation of the phenomenon transcends the situation: the one who does the speaking in tongues gets more out of it than those who listen unless the Spirit also provides an interpretation through someone in the assembly (or unless the hearer happens to understand the foreign, human tongue).

Paul also speaks of the Spirit bringing endowments of power to effect some dramatic changes in a person or situation. Paul expected the Spirit to work through Christians to extend healing to the sick or infirm. He expected works of power, probably including exorcism (which is actually still quite common in the majority world, especially Africa and Asia) and other manifestations that might promote receptivity to the gospel (as when Paul struck Elymas, a sorcerer and a rival, blind in the course of his preaching in Paphos). Of course, the faith required to step forward in these ways and know that God wants to see something done and wants to do it in response to *your* prayer—this is also a Spirit-endowed gift (see also Jas 5:14–18).

*   *   *

Most of us may have very little personal experience of these manifestations of the Spirit. Some of us may not be altogether certain that we would welcome such manifestations of the Spirit into our own lives, into our encounters with non-Christians, or into our congregational experience. It is my aim simply to elevate before you the witness of the apostles to this spiritual endowment that God supplies to God's church and to raise a question: Do we need to draw more fully on this spiritual endowment—not only in our own lives for our transformation but also in our congregation and in its work—so that God may attain God's ends more fully in our community? Are we interested in seeing our congregational resources, ministry, and witness reflect that of the assemblies in the New Testament and in plugging ourselves in more fully to the same source of direction and power? Or do we want to develop rationales for why our congregational life should *not* reflect the picture of Christian corporate life and ministry that we read therein?

If we were to read on to 1 Corinthians 13, we would come to what, for Paul, is the most essential, foundational, and lasting of Spirit-given endowments, namely the power to love—to be so centered in God's Spirit that one manifests patience, kindness, and forbearance in one's interactions and that one no longer manifests envy, arrogance, irritability, or resentment. And so Paul himself urged the Christians in Corinth, "Pursue love, *and* earnestly desire the spiritual gifts, especially that you may prophesy" (1 Cor 14:1), that you might become a mouthpiece for the Holy Spirit. We tend to take Paul quite seriously in regard to the rest of his advice. Perhaps we should here as well.

Obviously, moving out into these new waters would take careful preparation and skillful sailing. It would be essential that we grow in our rootedness in the Scripture as we grow in openness to the Spirit—ahead of growing in our exercise of the Spirit's gifts. The writings of the Old and New Testaments were not called an "anthology" but a "canon," the Greek word for a measuring stick, and this with good reason. Growing in openness to the Spirit and his gifts would also necessitate growing in spiritual maturity overall, not because God is going to endow us with some power that we might misuse but because we would need to equip ourselves with the self-knowledge and self-awareness that allows us to know the difference between our own voice and the Spirit's voice, our own impulses and the Spirit's impulses, our own capacity to mimic spiritual gifts and genuine expressions of the Spirit. Growing in *all* these areas, however, is a good and even a necessary thing regardless. And so I simply put it to you all: What should we do about this amazing endowment that God offers us, not as something that he makes available for *our* use but as something that makes us ever so much more available for *his* use?

16

"A New Pentecost" (Pentecost)

Acts 2:1–21, 38–39; Ephesians 5:15–20

We're probably all familiar with the idea of the "bucket list," even if we didn't see Jack Nicholson help Morgan Freeman create and then check the items off his own. Some of us may even have formalized such a list in writing. I haven't yet, though having gotten an estate plan for my fiftieth birthday I suspect that developing a bucket list might not be too far away for me in the natural course of things. The bucket list emerges from a person's confrontation with mortality—when a person realizes that the time left is limited and begins to think, "Wow! I haven't really done what I've wanted to do in this lifetime; I haven't gotten everything I wanted out of life." So one gets serious about sorting out what one will and will not get to do before the buzzer and begins to prioritize getting those things on the last pages of life's calendar.

It's unlikely that the person who is thus minded will list "open up more of myself and my life to God"; "get serious about investing myself in encouraging and supporting my sisters and brothers in Christ"; "seek out every opportunity to share Christ with others and plant the seeds of eternity in their hearts." But

Paul would urge his readers not to put even such rich activities on some bucket list but rather to start living life to the full—for eternity—today so that we have no need of a bucket list because we have made the most of our life all along the way.

> Take care how you live your life, that it not be as foolish people but as wise people, getting the most out of the time, because the days are evil. So don't be thoughtless, but understand what it is that the Lord wants. And don't get drunk on wine, which is a waste of your life, but let the Spirit fill you up as you recite psalms and hymns and spiritual songs among yourselves, singing and making music in your hearts to the Lord, giving thanks to the God and Father always and for everything in the name of our Lord Jesus Christ. (Eph 5:15-20)

Paul is dealing with topics of the utmost importance here—it's the difference between being foolish and being smart, between throwing away our lives and getting the most out of the limited span of our lives. If we're going to be smart, we need to "understand what it is that the Lord wants," and we need to invest the time that we have in the most profitable manner that we can.

Wine is a good example for Paul to call out here. We could extend this to any alcoholic beverages now, but the only options in the ancient world were wine and beer, with beer being much more of a fringe drink. Wine was a principal beverage throughout the Mediterranean, so Paul is not promoting teetotaling here. But he does warn against using wine for something other than a staple beverage, like using it to forget, using it to stupefy, or using it to fill the evenings and the empty spaces and going where it takes you.

But wine is only one vintage of a great many varietals of time-killers and space-fillers—whatever we turn to in order to pass the time, to numb ourselves, to fill the empty spaces, whether in our calendars or in our selves. Shopping. Just about anything on a television. Video games. Social media. Whatever you might use to fill the emptiness of a day and that leaves you feeling empty after you're done. It doesn't have to be just the obvious painkillers, distractions, and amusements. We can busy ourselves so much with day-to-day life and invest ourselves so much in questions and issues of fleeting importance that we are equally guilty of foolishness—of not getting the most for our time.

Paul warns us against going along with the flow in which the concerns and distractions of this world carry us along without our realizing that "the days are evil" and that the flow leads down toward the drain. Paul names the result of this way of life "dissipation"—by which he means "sheer waste," as in watching your energies, your resources, your time *dissipate*, evaporate, come to nothing. For Paul, whether we have been foolish or wise, whether we have indeed "made the most of the time" or thrown the time away, will be discovered from the kind of answer we can give at the end of the day to the questions: How does what I did with my day line up with what the Lord wants, be it *for* me or *from* me? Did how I lived out the day that is past, did the manner in which I spent all that time, grow out of a deep understanding of what the Lord wants (Eph 5:17)?

Paul has a good alternative in mind to all those time-killers and space-fillers: Don't fill up on those empty things; fill up on the Holy Spirit instead. Fill your head, fill your self-talk, fill your conversations with that which keeps your own focus and that of those around you on matters of eternal import. Fill your heart with the remembrance of what God has done for you and what God has yet prepared for you, so that your heart will feel how full God has made you and be stuffed with gratitude toward

God. Then you will be impelled into your day not by a hunger for empty things but by gratitude toward God, to discover and to do what the Lord wants to do in you and through you each and every day, with the Holy Spirit of God right there, dwelling with you, dwelling within you, animating you—giving you life in its fullness.

* * *

Today we celebrate Pentecost, the birthday of the church, the day on which the promised Holy Spirit came on the hundred and twenty Christ-followers and mobilized them to go out into the streets to proclaim the mighty acts of God surrounding Jesus' life, death, and rising again. The miracle of Pentecost was perfectly crafted for the diversity of the Jews and converts to Judaism gathered there, in the cosmopolitan city of Jerusalem. There were, no doubt, many Jews from around the diaspora that had relocated permanently to their mother city, but there was also an enormous swelling of the ranks of foreign Jews from throughout the Mediterranean during the three annual pilgrimage festivals. Passover had been the first of these; Pentecost was the second. The miracle was unmistakable, with all these pilgrims from every corner of the eastern Mediterranean hearing a bunch of Galileans shouting about the mighty acts of God in Chaldean, Lydian, Phrygian, Latin, Coptic, Mycenaean, and some precursor of Arabic. It was an attention-getting sign, to be sure, and it was pointing unambiguously to the fact that God was there doing something in the midst of Jesus' followers.

Pentecost was the name Greek-speaking Jews gave to the spring harvest festival (the first fruits of the grain harvest), which was also a celebration of God giving the Law, the Torah, to Israel on Mount Sinai. Pentecost comes from the Greek word for "fiftieth," since this festival was held on the fiftieth day after the first day of Passover. What happened on the fiftieth day after the Passover of Jesus' crucifixion, however, was a *new* Pentecost, the giving of the Holy Spirit in fulfillment of Israel's expectations of what would happen "in the last days." Peter quotes at length from the prophet Joel:

> I will pour out my Spirit upon all flesh,
>> and your sons and your daughters will prophesy,
> and the elders among you will dream dreams;
>> and your young ones will see visions.
> Yes, I will pour out my Spirit upon my slaves and my
>> maidservants. (Joel 2:28–29; compare
>> Acts 2:17–18)

The old Pentecost celebrated God's giving of the Law to regulate his people; this new Pentecost celebrated God's pouring out of the Holy Spirit to inspire his people with all manner of divine communication and guidance, and to empower them for righteousness and mission—indeed, to make himself wonderfully present in their midst and, through them, in the midst of the world.

I want to elevate two verses in particular as very important for us to hear this morning. When the crowds asked the disciples what they should do to fall in line with God, Peter answered straightforwardly: "Turn your life around and be baptized, each one of you, in the name of Jesus Christ for the forgiveness of your sins and receive the gift of the Holy Spirit, for this promise is for you and for your children and for all who are far off from here—for as many people as will call upon the Lord our God" (Acts 2:38–39).

In this one promise, the promise of the Spirit, are encapsulated a great many gifts.

The Spirit brings the power for you to know who you are in Christ and to know God's love and presence intimately, as intimately as we might know a father's love: "All who are led by the Spirit of God are children of God. ... You've received a spirit of adoption. When we cry, 'Abba! Father!' it is that very Spirit bearing witness with our spirit that we are God's children" (Rom 8:14-16). The Holy Spirit alive within us allows us to experience the intimate communion with God for which our souls yearn, into which God longs to draw us.

The Spirit also brings direction and power for living in alignment with God's righteousness, the power for a transformed life. "Live by the Spirit," Paul urges, "and you surely won't fulfill the desires to which your self-centered nature drives you." Rather than the "works of the flesh"—sexual impurity, idolatry, strife, jealousy, anger, quarrels, factions, and the like—our lives will show forth the Spirit's fruit—"love, joy, peace, patience, kindness, generosity, faithfulness, gentleness, and self-control" (Gal 5:13-25), with the result that we do from the heart what God's righteousness has always sought from us. The Spirit empowers us to stop contributing to the brokenness in the world because of sin and selfishness, working through us instead to contribute to God's redemptive activity wherever he moves us. It is this Spirit, coming alive within us and taking over within us, who allows us to live the kind of life that God will approve as righteous.

The Spirit brings power to build up other Christians as you become the instruments through which God encourages, counsels, and strengthens them (and they, you)!

To each is given the manifestation of the Spirit for the common good. To one is given through the Spirit the utterance of wisdom, and to another the utterance of knowledge according to the same Spirit, to another faith by the same Spirit, to another gifts of healing by the one Spirit, to another the working of miracles, to another prophecy, to another the discernment of spirits, to another various kinds of tongues, to another the interpretation of tongues. All these are activated by one and the same Spirit, who allots to each one individually just as the Spirit chooses. (1 Cor 12:7–11 NRSV)

The people around us in the congregation reach *their* full potential as disciples and as a community of disciples as *each* of us gives the Spirit freer rein to work through us for the others' encouragement, edification, and equipping. As a corollary, any *one* of us also depends on our neighbors' exercising the gifts that the Spirit wants to give them for the strengthening of the whole body of Christ.

And, of course, the Spirit brings power for effective witness. This was a major purpose highlighted by Jesus himself in the episodes prior to his ascension: "You will receive power when the Holy Spirit has come upon you; and you will be my witnesses in Jerusalem, in all Judea and Samaria, and to the ends of the earth" (Acts 1:8).

What a witness was borne on that day of Pentecost! And the disciples' witness is convincing and convicting because the Holy Spirit that drives the witnesses also moves upon those listening to their witness, and they join themselves to the community of Christ-followers by the thousands. The more we hear about the trials, tensions, and tragedies besetting people throughout our world, the more we must know that the people who are *not* in this sanctuary with us need this witness—and we need the Holy Spirit to drive us to bold witness *and* to make our witness effective for their sake.

* * *

In the midst of the Easter season, I invited us all to wait in our own metaphorical upper rooms with the expectancy of being clothed with power from on high. I invited you to pray to God about your receiving more of God's Holy Spirit yourself and about his releasing more of God's Spirit in our midst. Today, I want to invite the Holy Spirit to come upon us in a new Pentecost. I want to invite God to fan into flames what we have doused, to stoke the fires of the Spirit within us so that our hearts are not merely "strangely warmed" by our weekly visit with God but rather our whole lives are set ablaze by God's power at work within us and through us.

I want to invite you to surrender to God's desires for us. Here is where faith—trust—really comes into play. Open up to God with no negotiations, no bargaining, no parameters ("You can come in, Lord, as long as you don't do this or change that"). Just give yourselves over to live for him who died for us and rose again on our behalf, and let him pour his Holy Spirit—his very life—into you to live in and through you. In this way, I invite you to know all that God has for us, to experience and to become everything for which he has redeemed us, to do all that he wants to do through us for his church in every place and for the world.

I want to invite you, if you are willing, to a new Pentecost.

17

"The Arithmetic of God"
(Trinity Sunday)

Colossians 1:11–20; John 14:8–21

The first Sunday after Pentecost is also called "Trinity Sunday," and one morning a year is not too much to give to reflecting on the mystery of our creed—namely, that we worship only *one* God but worship this God as Father, Son, and Holy Spirit. This reflection is an important task given the fair amount of resistance out there to the traditional—the *orthodox*—understanding of a God who has made himself known in three distinct persons that, nevertheless, reveal *one* divine Being. The Trinity is not without its aggressive critics and detractors, who think that the traditional, orthodox Christian view of God is without merit—indeed, that it is a view unworthy of the One God.

Minds shaped by the Enlightenment, for example, have been quite hostile toward the idea of the Trinity. Thomas Jefferson represented many when he complained:

> When we shall have done away with the incomprehensible jargon of the Trinitarian arithmetic, that three are one, and one is three; when we shall have knocked down the artificial scaffolding, reared to mask from view the

very simple structure of Jesus; when, in short, we shall
have unlearned everything which has been taught since
his day, and got back to the pure and simple doctrines
he inculcated, we shall then be truly and worthily
his disciples.[1]

His legacy continues in a number of forms, including much of
the "quest for the historical Jesus"—the search for the *man* from
Nazareth who could serve as the true center for a new Christianity stripped of all the doctrinal encrustation that had accumulated around him and obscured him from view.

Resistance to the Trinity began long before the Enlightenment, however. Jehovah's Witnesses, true sons and daughters of
the third-century deacon Arius, who taught that the Son of God
was just a created being like the angels and was not eternal since
he had a definite beginning, periodically come to my door promoting that ancient heresy. I use the word "heresy" here in its
fullest sense—not merely a divergent opinion about some religious topic, but a faction, a divisive movement that has broken
away from the larger church on account of its commitment to
its divergent opinion and uses the ongoing promotion of that
divergent opinion as its very reason to exist as a separate sect.

Most dramatically, there are a billion people in this world
who read, as their sacred Scripture, a collection of pronounce-
ments that include the following:

O People of the Book! Do not exaggerate in your religion
nor utter anything concerning Allah save the truth. The
Messiah, Jesus son of Mary, was only a messenger of
Allah. ... So believe in Allah and His messengers, and say
not "Three"—Cease! (it is) better for you!—Allah is only

---

1. Letter to Timothy Pickering, February 27, 1821.

One God. Far be it removed from His transcendent majesty that he should have a son. (*Surah* 4:171)

Lo! whoever assigns partners to Allah, to him Allah has forbidden Paradise. His abode will be the Fire. ... They are infidels who say, "Lo! Allah is the third of three," when there is no God save the One God. (*Surah* 5:72–73)

I am not enough of a theologian to present an airtight case for the Trinity nor explain it even to my own satisfaction, but I am nevertheless convinced that the orthodox Christian position does greater justice to the evidence of our own Scriptures than any other. It is my goal in this brief amount of time to share with you *why* I remain unpersuaded by the Jehovah's Witnesses at my door, the impatient child of the Enlightenment at a scholarly conference, or by the voice of Muhammad himself.

* * *

I am unpersuaded by these critics, first, because I accept the limitations of my own mind in regard to grasping the arithmetic of God, rather than limit the arithmetic of God to what my own mind can grasp. If we are to ponder God as Trinity, we should first accept that there is no analogy based on anything in the created, natural order that will suffice to exemplify the Trinity. There are good analogies for *features* of the Trinity, but the absolute difference in category of being—that which constitutes God versus that which constitutes "all [created] things, seen and unseen"—renders it categorically impossible to find anywhere in our experience in this world an analogy that will capture the Trinity absolutely. We must be content, as even Paul had to remain content, that "now we see in a polished metal mirror, dimly, but then we shall see face-to-face; now I know in part; then I shall know fully, even as I am fully known" (1 Cor 13:12).

Gregory of Nazianzus, a fourth-century bishop, cautions us even more eloquently concerning how we ought to set our expectations for knowing God. Gregory recalls Moses' desire to see God, with God granting Moses' request to the extent that Moses would be able to endure the sight. The story can be found in Exodus 33:18-23. Placing Moses in a large fissure in a rock, God covers Moses' eyes until God has passed by, allowing Moses only to see God's back. Gregory reasons from this that he, too, will not perceive "the absolute and pure divine nature, known only to the Trinity itself," but only "that part of the divine nature that at last reaches us, the degree of glory that can be shown to God's creatures. These are the back parts of God, which he leaves behind him as tokens of himself, like the reflections of the sun in the water, which show the sun to our weak eyes, because we cannot look at the sun itself, for by his unmixed light he is too strong for our power of perception."[2] The traditional, orthodox view of God starts there, really, in the traces of God left behind in our experience—and that experience includes encountering God as Father, the creator of all that is; God as Son, the redeemer of all that is and the revelation of who God is by virtue of his incarnation; and God as Holy Spirit, the transforming divine presence within us and among us.

I dwell on this point because it is a major failure of critics of the Trinity that they insist on limiting discussion of God's Being to what can be grasped by their minds—and thus that 1 + 1 + 1 *must* equal 3 gods, which they can't accept, so neither will they think of God as Son or God as Holy Spirit, for if they are to have one God, they can only conceive of that God as one person—the Father, by default. If we insist on limiting our conception of God to what our minds can clearly comprehend, we place undue

2. *Second Theological Oration*, adapted.

limits on God, the knowledge of whom *by definition* exceeds our minds' capacity.

The Christian Scriptures loudly proclaim monotheism, in concert with our parent religion, Judaism, whose foundational creed is heard in Deuteronomy: "Listen, Israel: The LORD our God is God alone" (Deut 6:4). God's self-revelation through the prophet Isaiah is also distinctly monotheistic: "Before me no god was formed, nor shall there be any after me" (Isa 43:10); "I am the first and I am the last; besides me there is no god" (Isa 44:6). At the same time, our Scriptures speak of the worship of Christ—indeed, the worship *due* Christ—as, in some sense, himself divine. After Thomas encounters the risen Jesus, he exclaims, "My Lord and my God!" (John 20:28), acknowledging that the divine is truly present in the man before him. Paul speaks of Jesus' place in the cosmos in similar terms at the end of his hymn to Christ in Philippians 2: "God super-exalted him and graced him with the name that is above every name"—the divine name!—"in order that, at the name of Jesus, every knee of heavenly and earthly and subterranean beings should bend and every tongue acknowledge that Jesus Christ is Lord, unto the Father's glory" (Phil 2:9–11). The universal worship of Jesus as "Lord," the title that replaced the not-to-be-spoken proper name of God throughout the Old Testament, does not detract from the worship of God (as it would, were Jesus a second god or an idol) but glorifies the Father as well. The clear legacy of our sacred Scriptures is that we worship one God *and* that we worship Christ as divine, which still means, however, glorifying the One God.

Detractors will complain that the word "Trinity" does not appear in the Bible, which is true enough. And finding Father, Son, and Holy Spirit all together at a number of points throughout Scripture does not yet mean "Trinity" but only names the three persons that later Christians will confess to be one God known in these three persons. But faithful reflection on the statements that *do* appear in the Bible regarding the oneness of God, the relationship of the Father and the Son, and the work of the Holy Spirit lead by a rather direct path in that direction.

Our reading from the Gospel according to John is one such statement:

> Philip said to Jesus, "Lord, show us the Father, and it will suffice for us." Jesus said to him, "Have I been with you for so long and you don't know me, Philip? The one who has seen me has seen the Father! How can you say, 'Show us the Father'? Don't you trust that I am in the Father and the Father is in me?" (John 14:8–10)

For Jesus to say that seeing him is the equivalent of seeing the Father more than suggests some basic identity between the Father and the Son—indeed, Jesus had affirmed an essential identity just a few chapters earlier when he declared, "I and the Father are one" (John 10:30), or, a bit more enigmatically here, "I am in the Father and the Father is in me." John began his Gospel in a way that foregrounded this very theme: "The Word was God ... and the Word became flesh and dwelt in our midst" (John 1:1, 14). Here is an implicit analogy: the relationship between the Father and the Son is like the relationship between a speaker and what is spoken. What is spoken is inseparable from the speaker; it proceeds from the speaker but is not some manufactured, independent product of the speaker; it emerges from the speaker into the environment to be experienced by others, even as the Word emerged from the Father into the visible world as Jesus, the Word-made-flesh, to be experienced by others. Nevertheless, the implicit analogy also shows its inadequacy because, in human (rather than divine) experience, our speech does not remain a part of us, does not have life equal to our own. John's point, however, remains: something of the One God became a human being and, by so doing, revealed the One God in a new way in the world.

*   *   *

Paul's lofty words about Christ in Colossians echo this point when, after speaking about the Father rescuing us and transferring us into the kingdom of his Son, Paul speaks of the Son as "the image of the unseen God" (Col 1:15). We might be tempted to think of Christ as the image of God in a manner analogous to the way human beings were created in the image of God, but I think Paul is going in a quite different direction here. People in the Greco-Roman world often referred to what we would call an "idol" as the "image" of the god. Images provided physical representations of unseen gods—the idol *wasn't* the god insofar as it was a handcrafted object, but it also *was* the god insofar as worship offered to the image was offered in fact to the god. The genuine God—the *living* God—could not, Paul knew, be represented by any such graven image, a lifeless thing. But Paul can point to Christ as a living image of the living God—not some part of material creation masquerading as a god (which is what every stone or bronze or wooden idol was) but the projection into the visible realm of the one, genuine, living God—God the Son made visible in his incarnation.

Paul continued by calling Christ "the firstborn of all creation." This was a verse that Arius treasured, reading "firstborn of all creation" as a sign that the Son is himself a part of creation. He ignored, however, the more likely sense here of "firstborn over all creation,"[3] since the Son himself helps to bring all creation, every creature, into being, as Paul immediately goes on to say: "because, in him, all things in heaven and upon the earth, things visible and invisible, were created—whether thrones or dominions or rulers or authorities, all things were created through him and for him. He is prior to all things and all things hold together in him. ... In him all the fullness was pleased to dwell" (1:15–17, 19).

If that last clause sounds enigmatic, Paul circles back to spell it out more fully just a few paragraphs later: "In Christ all the fullness of the Deity dwelt in bodily form" (2:9). And yet, the *totality* of deity was not contained in—that is, limited to—the six feet of body that was Jesus of Nazareth, for the Father was still active in the world and the Holy Spirit still operative beyond Jesus. Thus, the early fathers of the church reasoned, the Word, the Son, who was fully God but not the totality of God, became flesh—a distinct person of the Trinity who could refer to himself as "Son," still refer to and speak to God as "Father," and still work in the world by the Holy Spirit.

* * *

Congregations, it seems, tend to like the Apostles' Creed more than the Nicene Creed—possibly because it is shorter, and reciting it doesn't require us to stand as long; possibly because it is missing a lot of the metaphysical language about the Son that seems remote to us. The Nicene Creed, however, contains some careful language crafted to keep us thinking worthily of the Son in particular. The phrases "eternally begotten of the Father, God from God, light from light, genuine God from genuine God,

3. The genitive case is capable of conveying a wide array of potential relationships between the noun in the genitive case and the noun that governs it, subordination being one.

begotten, *not* made" reflect the early church's decisive rejection of Arius's claims concerning Jesus—namely, that there was a time when the Son was not and that the Son was a created being. Those who formulated the creed reasoned that the Father could not eternally have been "Father" were the "Son" not also eternal. Gregory of Nazianzus explains: "Can one imagine the sun as existing apart from the light rays it constantly emits? The rays find their source, their origin, in the sun, but the rays and the sun also came into existence at the same time." Emitting light is simply in the nature of being a star. Begetting God the Son is simply in the nature of God the Father.

The phrase that claims the Son to be "of one 'Being' [of one 'Substance'] with the Father" affirms that the Son is like the Creator, not like the creation. The Son shares whatever it is that constitutes the One God. Athanasius, another fourth-century theologian, explains: "The sun's rays truly belong to it, but the sun's substance is not divided or diminished by its extending its rays. The rays do not diminish the substance of the light but are a true offspring of it. In a similar fashion we understand that the Son is begotten not from something external to the Father but from the Father himself."[4] Hence the Son is "God from God, Light from Light, genuine God from genuine God."

The fathers of the church gave such energy and care to these discussions because they rightly perceived the implications for the gospel itself. Do we understand that our redemption is fundamentally God's own work on our behalf, or do we think it's the work of a third party, some created emissary who took the fall for us? Do we believe that we really see the invisible Father in the person and work of Jesus? Is Jesus as "incarnate Son" really our surest glimpse of the invisible God's mind, heart, and will?

4. *Oration against the Arians* 2.24, 33 (my translation).

The theological refinements of the Nicene Creed sought to preserve these basic scriptural affirmations, which stand at the very foundations of our faith.

Having offered four sermons on the Holy Spirit, I may be forgiven for giving the Spirit short shrift here. I'll simply note that, in our Gospel reading, Jesus can call the Spirit both "*another* Advocate"—distinct from himself—and, at the same time, the vehicle by which the Son will not leave his followers orphaned, but rather come to be present with them (John 14:16-18). And so we speak in our creed of the Holy Spirit, "who proceeds from the Father and the Son," who comes to us out from both while also carrying along both to us. The last verse of our Gospel reading suggests that this is a Trinity that reaches out to embrace and include us as well. Jesus says: "In that day"—that is, the day in which we receive the Spirit—"you will know that I am in my Father and that you are in me and that I am in you" (14:20). The first statement pertains to knowing the Trinity, but the second pertains to our knowing ourselves to have been embraced fully by the Trinity— and it is ultimately only as we live more and more in that embrace that we will come to know God as insiders ourselves.

18

"A Surprisingly Satisfying Spread" (World Communion Sunday)

Exodus 12:1–11, 24–28;
1 Corinthians 11:23–26; John 6:48–58

O ur rite of Holy Communion has to be mystifying to outsiders. This is a lot of hoopla over a tiny cube of bread and a quick dip of the same into some grape juice. It's even more difficult to understand at the late service, by which time these cubes of bread have essentially become croutons. And yet, month after month, we delay our enjoyment of boxes of doughnuts and trays of baked goods for at least ten extra minutes so that we can come to *this* table and receive *this* cube of bread and dip of grape juice.

In terms of physical nourishment, this act does next to nothing for us. But, received as spiritual nourishment, it is, in the words of Thomas à Kempis, "the health of soul and body, the cure of every spiritual malady. By it, our vices are cured, our passions restrained, temptations are lessened, grace is given in fuller measure, and virtue once established is fostered; faith is confirmed, hope is strengthened, and love kindled and deepened."[1] It is not the simple act of receiving bread and grape juice, of course, that provides such a remarkable litany of spiritual benefits but receiving the promises and gifts of God that have been joined to this bread and this wine and, in particular, the intimate contact with Jesus that the rite facilitates. I want to make sure that our expectations for this encounter are raised sufficiently high. We shouldn't be afraid to expect too much from Holy Communion, for this is a feast that has the potential *always* to exceed our expectations for it; we should be afraid to expect too little, lest we not prepare ourselves adequately for what God wishes to do in us and among us through it, lest we miss out because we weren't looking for it.

* * *

A sacrament can be defined as the outward and visible sign of an inward and invisible gift from God[2]—we might say a divine promise joined to a physical sign, whether the water of baptism or the bread and cup of Holy Communion. In our reading from Paul's First Letter to the Corinthians—the earliest written documentation of that last night—Jesus takes the cup and says, "This cup is the new covenant in my blood." A promise is joined to the cup and the drinking of its contents, the promise of the "new covenant" announced by God in Jeremiah 31:31–34, the only passage in the Old Testament to use the expression.

---

1. *The Imitation of Christ*, book 4, chapter 4.

2. As in the catechism of *The Book of Common Prayer*, p. 857. The definition is held to be derived ultimately from Augustine's view of the sacraments. See T. F. Torrance, "The One Baptism Common to Christ and His Church," in *Theology in Reconciliation: Essays towards Evangelical and Catholic Unity in East and West* (Great Britain: Geoffrey Chapman, 1975), 95.

There God promises to "make a new covenant with the house of Israel and the house of Judah." This will differ from the first covenant in that God will "put [his] law within them, and ... write it on their hearts," and it is accompanied by the promise that God "will forgive their iniquity and remember their sin no more." Jesus' death changes God's perception of us as well as our perception of our own standing before God. As we receive the bread and the cup, we appropriate afresh the promise attached to this new covenant, that God "will remember our sins no more." We can enter God's presence—now in worship, hereafter for eternity—with full confidence of being accepted by God and finding favor with him.

We come to this table to *remember*. Remembering Jesus' giving of himself to us and for us is so important that it is given repeated attention in the words of institution both as found in the New Testament and as used in many Communion liturgies. "This is my body, which is given for you. *Do this in remembrance of me*" (Luke 22:19). "This cup is the new covenant in my blood. *Do this*, as often as you drink it, *in remembrance of me*" (1 Cor 11:25). At this table, we fix our gaze intently on Jesus' self-giving as one of the principal compass points by means of which we chart our course toward newness of life. Remembering again and again the cost of the forgiveness of our past sins, underwritten by Jesus with such great love for us and such passion to restore us to God, means that we will not so casually allow ourselves to fall back into the ruts of the old person. Jesus died so that we would leave those well-worn paths behind.

Remembering also ensures that we will keep focused on *responding* gratefully to Jesus before all else. Every time we return to this table to hear again the story of Jesus' giving of himself for us, the answer to the question "How then shall we live?" is clarified. We shall live in such a way as honors Jesus' costly love for us and death on our behalf. We will live in such a way as moves us forward into the life with God that was Jesus' goal for us as he stretched out his arms upon the cross. Forgetting is the great danger to our souls. Forgetting is precisely what the world, the flesh, and the devil seek to make us do as they seek to fill our consciousness with their distractions and clamor, so that we will respond to their noise rather than to Jesus in his self-giving love. The simple act of remembering—and remembering often—stands at the foundation of our ongoing spiritual formation.

But we come to the table not only to *remember* Jesus but also to *encounter* Jesus. We become present to Jesus and his self-giving love on the night before his passion, while Jesus becomes present to us in our churches as we, too, gather around a table. In Holy Communion, the two horizons of these two tables merge. The fact that the Last Supper was a Passover meal is significant: the Jews' annual celebration of Passover involved telling the story of their ancestors' deliverance, over the sharing of flat bread, roasted lamb, and bitter herbs, which gave each person the opportunity to regard himself or herself as if he or she also had come forth from Egypt. Generation after generation, practicing Jews experience that foundational event not as distant viewers but as participants, saying, "*We* were slaves in Egypt." *They,* and not just their ancestors, were delivered by God from slavery in Egypt. It is with *them* that God has made a covenant. *They* must now respond faithfully to God as those who have experienced God's deliverance.

In a similar fashion, when *we* tell the story of Jesus' giving of himself to his disciples and share bread and wine, we become present with Jesus on the night on which he gave himself. The words of institution transport us back to the place where Jesus offered himself to his disciples. We share the table with the Lord acting as our host, breaking bread and offering the cup, creating fellowship over the sharing of food. Now Jesus is offering the bread and the cup to *us* who gather around the table of the altar. Jesus holds out the bread and the cup to us, and says, "My body, given for you; my blood, shed for you," allowing us to receive and appropriate for ourselves his enormous expression of love. We take the bread, hearing not just that "Christ died for many," but that "Christ died for *you*," for you in particular, for me in particular. We don't merely see pastors, Communion servers, tiny squares of bread, and the other paraphernalia here; we see Jesus "offering us his own body and blood to preserve our bodies and souls to everlasting life."[3] Even though we were not present in body at the crucifixion, we grasp that we were present in Jesus' heart, intentions, and embrace—an embrace we experience in the sacrament. And like our spiritual ancestors who celebrated their Passover, we, too, have experienced a deliverance. Christ *our* Passover died to break the power of *our* captors—sin, death, the structures of this world, and Satan—so that we may live a life beyond their oppressive rule over us.

The layers of mystery continue, however, as Jesus our host, to whom we have become present, becomes the feast. Our connection with Jesus grows deeper as we go from sitting at the table with him to the mystical taking of Christ into our very selves. As we heard from John's Gospel, Jesus is remembered to have said, "I am the living bread that came down from heaven. ... Those who eat my flesh and drink my blood have eternal life, and I will raise them up on the last day. ... Those who eat my flesh and drink my blood abide in me, and I in them" (John 6:51, 54, 56). Jesus attaches these promises to the visible and outward

---

3. William Beveridge, *The Great Necessity and Advantage of Public Prayer and Frequent Communion* (Chichester: Wm. Mason, 1840), 269–70.

sign of eating this bread and drinking from this cup. Jesus does not simply come to be "with us" in the sacrament. He comes to infuse us with himself, to take on flesh anew in us as his body, the church, to so unite us with himself as to bring us at last to the point where we can say with Paul, "It is no longer I who live, but it is Christ who lives in me" (Gal 2:20). This is a feast at which we truly *become* what we eat, and what we eat *takes over* who we are, to our ultimate salvation.

And it is here that we come back to the promise of God in the new covenant of Jeremiah—not merely that God would remember our sins no more but would put his law in our hearts. For the early Christians, this was the role undertaken by the Holy Spirit, God's promised gift that would enable his people to discern his instruction in the doing of his will day by day, thus to fulfill what the law was after all along. The promise of the new covenant assures us that God indeed supplies all that is necessary for us to enter into and walk consistently in newness of life as we follow the leading of the Holy Spirit that God has sent into our hearts—the Spirit that breathes the life of Jesus into us, that causes Jesus to take shape within us and to live through us.

But there is yet another dimension to Holy Communion that we dare not neglect—the other people around the table. Holy Communion is an expression not only of our being joined inwardly to Christ but also of our being knit together with one another into the *people* of the new covenant: "Because there is one bread, we who are many are one body, for we all partake from the one bread" (1 Cor 10:17). The unity of the loaf—which is Christ—remains intact, no matter how widely he is distributed in the bread and the cup. As Christ takes on flesh and blood in each one of us, he takes on flesh and blood in *all* of us collectively, unifying us into a single body. There can be no receiving of Christ without receiving one another as sisters and brothers who have also taken Christ's life into their lives. I would encourage you, after you receive the bread and the cup, to pay attention to your sisters and brothers in the congregation. They are part of the body to which you have been joined. Ask God to open your heart more and more to each person, especially those toward whom you have some aversion. Ask him to help you release whatever in *you* threatens the unity and solidarity of the body.

* * *

This meal, however, is also just an appetizer. Looking to Jesus on the night before his suffering and death must cause us also to look ahead to the consummation of his self-giving death, when his death for the life of the world will have achieved its full and final effect. Jesus pointed in this direction at his Last Supper with his disciples. After offering them the cup, he announced, "Truly I tell you, I will never again drink of the fruit of the vine until that day when I drink it new in the kingdom of God" (Mark 14:25). Paul kept this focus alive, reminding us in our epistle reading that "as often as you eat this bread and drink the cup, you proclaim the Lord's death until he comes" (1 Cor 11:26).

Therefore we, too, continue to proclaim our hope in the context of the Great Thanksgiving. We look backward: "Christ has died; Christ is risen." But we also look forward: "Christ will come again."[4] Looking back to our cleansing from sin impels us forward to grow in grace and equip ourselves with all the virtues God seeks to nurture within and among us; looking ahead to Christ's final victory draws us forward on the same trajectory.

---

4. *The Book of Common Prayer and Administration of the Sacraments and Other Rites and Ceremonies of the Church together with The Psalter or Psalms of David According to the use of the Episcopal Church* (New York: The Church Hymnal Corporation, 1979), 363.

The regular practice of Holy Communion can be likened to the practice of the premodern sea captain, who would come out from his cabin at regular intervals throughout the night with his sextant and take his bearings from a fixed star on the one hand and the horizon on the other, to discover his position and certify that he was still on course. The more frequently we set before our eyes the death of Jesus on our behalf on the one hand and the coming again of Jesus in glory to judge the living and the dead on the other, the more likely we are to remain on course as we navigate the challenging waters of our lives in this world.

All this is here for us in the bread and the cup, because Christ himself is here with us, giving himself to us and drawing us into himself in this bread and this cup. Amen.

19

"Who's Watching You Run?" (All Saints)

Hebrews 12:1–3

Today we celebrate the Feast of All Saints. Protestant Christians, I have observed, tend to be uncomfortable when it comes to "saints." "Saints" belong to our Roman Catholic sisters and brothers—or to our Anglican and Episcopalian sisters and brothers who like to *think* they're Protestant but really aren't. Their churches are named after saints. Their churches are adorned with images of saints. Their liturgies speak of living worshipers joining their prayers with the prayers of "all the saints" who have gone before, who make intercession for us who still struggle in faith on this nearer side of death. This, in turn, only increases Protestant discomfort around "saints," since there are still some pretty strong boundary issues between many Protestant and Catholic Christians.

Besides (as I've often heard Protestants claim when they object to singling out certain persons as saints), aren't we *all* saints? Don't the New Testament Scriptures consistently speak of all the redeemed together as God's saints, God's "holy ones" (e.g., Rom 1:7; 15:26; 16:15; 2 Cor 1:1; Eph 1:1, 15; 5:3)? Doesn't the practice of singling out certain people as "saints" who are more especially worthy of remembrance and attention violate the democratic ideal of the people of God? Perhaps, but let's face it: Christ shines through *some* saints far more clearly and brightly than through others. In this life in which we are constantly searching for reliable models of what Christ looks like when he takes on flesh afresh in his servants—of what it looks like when it is no longer a particular person who is living, but Christ who is living *through* that person (Gal 2:19-20)—identifying those people through whom Christ shines most brightly, most transparently, is of great value (2 Cor 4:7).

I think it's also very important that such saints be dead. While we live, it is always possible for the light of Christ shining within us to be shrouded by some failure in the face of temptation, to be all but extinguished by some suddenly manifested sin or act that all at once calls into question the integrity of our witness. How dangerous it is to allow oneself to be inspired by a mortal who, tomorrow, can become a witness to worldliness, the power of sin, the play acting of hypocrisy! But those "whom the faithful seal of death has perfected" (4 Macc 7:15), who have lived *and died* in the faith and with the radiance of Christ undiminished in their lives, who show us that the race *can* be run well to the end—these can light our way reliably rather than suddenly leaving us in the dark and liable to stumble ourselves.

* * *

So what are we, good Protestants that we are, to do with saints? Nothing more and nothing less, really, than the author of the Letter to the Hebrews did with his saints. What he did—in that chapter with which we may be familiar as "the faith chapter," Hebrews 11—was to decorate the walls of the audience's minds with poster after poster of *their* saints, the exemplary figures of the Jewish Scriptures who had received God's promises and kept walking toward them, even if they tripped up a bit here and there, without allowing anything to turn them aside from obedient faith. If the author of Hebrews had had a video projector and multiple screens, he would have flashed up pictures of Noah, Abraham, Moses, the great prophets, the Maccabean-era martyrs, and all the other familiar saints who showed what faith looks like in action—how faith thinks, how faith weighs decisions, how faith assesses temporal situations, how faith prioritizes, how faith behaves. If we are to be people of faith, he tells his hearers, we need to become more like those who lived as people of faith, so here's what they looked like and what we need to learn in order to embody the same virtue and arrive at the same goal God intends for them and for us.

Noah teaches us that, when God announces his intention to hold the world accountable, the smartest thing to do is to leave off living "life as usual" and invest fully in a plan to survive that accounting. Abraham teaches us that attaining what God has promised is well worth leaving behind everything familiar, everything comfortable, everything that gives us our place in this world. Moses teaches us that solidarity with God's oppressed people is of greater value and honor than the enjoyment of the palaces of the oppressor. The prophets teach us that God's word of promise and of warning to this generation must be boldly spoken, whatever the consequences to the messengers.

And so, with his audience's mind freshly populated with these and two dozen other examples, the author writes:

> Therefore, since we indeed have so great a cloud of witnesses surrounding us, let us put every burden off to the side and strip off the sin that hampers our movements like a close-fitting garment, and let us run with endurance the race course that has been laid out in front of

us. And let us do this with our eyes fixed ahead on Jesus,
faith's pioneer and perfecter. For the sake of the joy set
out in front of him, he endured a cross, despising shame,
and has sat down at the right hand of God's throne. Consider him who endured such great opposition against
himself from sinful people, so that you may not lose heart
or grow weary in your souls. (Heb 12:1-3)

The author sets us down on the field of a stadium, and the stands
are filled with the saints who have gone before—now not only
the Old Testament worthies, but almost two millennia of Christian saints who have devoted their lives to seeking out the prize
of Christ's heavenward call. We are not competing here in our
wrestling matches against sin or in the race for the heavenly
prize (which often no doubt feels more like jumping hurdles
than a straight run!) in front of crowds of flaccid spectators,
but in front of crowds of successful, retired athletes—Olympic
winners, every one of them. We are accustomed to thinking of
the "witnesses" in this cloud (12:1) as people who testify to something, mostly to the value of God's promises and therefore of the
value of walking in line with faith even though it costs one's life.
Indeed, the heroes of faith celebrated in Hebrews 11, along with
a great number of Christian saints, *do* bear this testimony—
that living faithfully before God, that investing ourselves first
and fully in responding to God's call, is always advantageous
for us, no matter what its temporal costs. But here the author
of Hebrews has arrayed these saints as witnesses of a different
sort: they are spectators witnessing how well *we* are engaging
the same challenges and the same pursuit that they have completed engaging and in which they have triumphed.

Who is watching *us* run? The confessors of the church—
those who suffered everything short of death for their

testimony to Jesus—watch us when we are unwilling to suffer even a moment's awkwardness in order to testify to God's goodness and Jesus' deliverance. The martyrs who died for their devotion to remaining faithful and obedient to their Savior watch us when we are reluctant even to suffer inconvenience for the sake of obeying and claiming our Lord. The apostles watch us as we water down their challenge and adulterate their vision for the church and for committed Christian discipleship, all in the hope of appealing to our audiences by making "being a Christian" less intrusive and demanding upon our everyday lives. Francis of Assisi and Mother Teresa watch us as we turn away from a poor person. Augustine watches us as we fail to search our minds and hearts for the ways in which our desires have led us astray from God. John Wesley and Martin Luther King, Jr. watch us as we fail to make social justice and social holiness an integral part of our life's work and the work of our congregation. Dietrich Bonhoeffer watches us as we peddle the cheap grace that makes salvation another commodity rather than a demand for a life of radical obedience. And so on.

*　　*　　*

The author of Hebrews wants three things for us as we stand in the stadium his words have erected around us. The first is a healthy sense of shame before the generations of the faithful in Christ who have gone before. Those who have run the race of faith successfully are watching us, how well we run. Shouldn't we be more concerned to run our course well so as to be applauded by them, to live up to their expectations and example, than to live within the expectations of those around us, many of whom remain oblivious to God's call? This is one of the central features of the author's climactic example of faith-in-action, the one whom we see in the most prominent box seat overhanging rows of other seats—*Jesus*.

Hebrews 12:2 is a verse that some major translations, starting with the King James Version, have simply gotten wrong. The New Revised Standard Version, which I generally love, presents Jesus as "the pioneer and perfecter of *our* faith" (the ESV, NLT, and 1984 version of the NIV also include "our"). But there's no "our" in the Greek text, and the usual signals for understanding an "our" to be implied are simply not there. The 2011 revision of the NIV and the CEB get it right: Jesus is "the pioneer and perfecter of faith" itself. We can look to Noah, Abraham, and Moses for great examples of faith-in-action, but no one has gone further into the territory of living faithfully toward God and faithfully investing in God's promises than Jesus—hence he is faith's "pioneer." He is also the one in whom faith-in-action shows itself most completely—hence he is faith's "perfecter," our best and fullest example of faith-in-action.

If Jesus was to arrive at the honor set before him, an honor to be enjoyed forever before God's court of opinion, it was necessary for him to despise shame with respect to the human court of opinion, that court that regarded him worthy of execution as a criminal and subjected him to the greatest degradation then available on account of his obedience to God's call. The author of Hebrews wants us to have a sense of shame *lest* we fail to go the distance for Jesus that he was willing to go for us. And so he writes as he wraps up his own sermon: "Jesus, in order to make the people holy by means of his own blood, also suffered outside of the city gate; so now let *us* keep moving out of the camp and out toward him, bearing the reproach that he bore. For our lasting city isn't *here*, but we are looking expectantly for the one that is coming" (Heb 13:12–14).

* * *

But the second thing the author of Hebrews wants for us is to see these saints cheering us on—by their words and examples, by their hearts that, in life, fervently wished for other disciples to run as well, if not better, than they themselves had done, and perhaps now even from beyond death so wish for us. We are connected to these saints. The body of Christ spans time just as surely as it spans place. It is not cut in two by death, over which Christ has triumphed. And we can and should look regularly into the stands and be inspired in our race as we remember the victories won by this or that particular saint who ran the race well to the end and received the victor's crown.

Christ's work is not restricted to the pages of the Gospels or the New Testament as a whole. For a little less than two thousand years, Christ has continued working, and the testimony to this work is to be read in the lives and seen in the demeanor and practices of the saints. The saints are witnesses to the fact that transformation can in fact happen and are examples drawn in flesh and blood of how to recognize and seek transformation. For those who like to read stories about people, there is a whole genre devoted to "lives of the saints." You can learn about any number of hundreds of Christians who discovered how to live out God's calling in their lives, who overcame challenges similar to our own, who discerned *and made* their contribution to the ongoing work of building God's kingdom. Let their stories and their discoveries inspire and guide your own.

And let us also bear in mind that the event taking place in the stadium of faith is also a kind of relay race. The saints of yesterday have run well and now have taken their places in the winners' circle that simultaneously surrounds us. But the event itself is not over. Rather, the contest has been entrusted by these saints to us in our generation. We have a faith on the basis of which to run only because of the witness and nurture of saints who have gone before us, who were faithful to their own calling in their generation. The day will come when we, hopefully, will be gathered into that cloud of witnesses. Will we be able to watch people running whose place on the field *we* have helped to secure? Will we be able to watch saints competing whom *we* have recruited for the Lord's events? The activity that continues on this field after our passing will happen because saints in *our* generation have recruited and trained saints for a new generation, to recruit and train, in their turn, saints for yet another generation, and so on until the Master of the Games returns to the field.

*   *   *

So I would venture to suggest that a third thing that the author of Hebrews wants for us to feel is *weight*—the weight first of the wholehearted investment of themselves that two millennia of Christian saints have given to the proclamation and living of the gospel of Christ's lordship and, therefore, the weight of responsibility for the ongoing proclamation and living of the same that has fallen upon the church of *this present* generation. For they were not running only for themselves, but for us, who are gathered in churches throughout the world this day because of their witness and work; their torch has been passed now to us, together with all our sisters and brothers in Christ throughout the world, to run now not only for ourselves (as we also *must*) but also for the next generation of saints whom we must diligently summon and train for Christ's kingdom, so that Christ will continue to have a body in this world that will continue his redeeming work for generations to come.

Therefore, since we indeed have so great a cloud of witnesses surrounding us, let us put every burden off to the side and strip off the sin that hampers our movements like a close-fitting garment, and let us run with endurance the race course that has been laid out in front of us. And let us do this with our eyes fixed ahead on Jesus, faith's pioneer and perfecter.

Amen.

20

"Just Remember Who's Boss" (Christ the King)

Colossians 1:9–20; Luke 6:46–49

*T*oday is Christ the King Sunday, the climax and end of the liturgical calendar that starts afresh the following Sunday with Advent. We Americans, however, don't have the best history with kings and with being part of a kingdom. Remember King George III? The Revolutionary War, also called the War for *Independence*? We prize self-determination, self-direction, autonomy in as many areas of life as we can get it. We prize the freedom to do our own thing, to live as we want, to follow our own desires, and pursue our own dreams and goals. Unlike Christmas—for which Target, Wal-Mart, the local mall, and the neighbor across the street from me have already decorated— Christ the King Sunday is a fairly un-American event in the liturgical calendar. In John's story of Jesus' trial, the Judeans could cry out against him, "We have no king but Caesar!" We, however, would simply shout out, "We have no king! Period!" Our ideal is to be able to say: "I'm my *own* boss!"

Paul's political context, however, was empire, essentially a single kingdom built out of a dozen originally independent kingdoms that had been absorbed or otherwise subdued. At the

170

center of this megakingdom was the Roman emperor, a son of deified emperors dead and gone. There was no representative democracy. What this one man decided, generally in consultation with about six hundred of the richest of the richest men in Rome, was what happened.

Paul makes a pretty radical statement, then, both about life under the Roman emperors and about the political significance of conversion to Christianity when he says: "God has rescued us from the authority of darkness and transferred us into the kingdom of his beloved Son" (Col 1:13). First, Paul makes an assertion here that the age of Emperor Augustus and his successors is not some return to a "golden age," as the Roman court poets and propagandists trumpeted throughout the empire. It's not an expression of the loving care of beneficent deities. No, says Paul, this was the time when the power of darkness held sway—when God's *enemies* were in the driver's seat. Paul also asserts that conversion to Christ means joining a new political entity with new allegiances, even while still living in the middle of the kingdom of darkness and its rulers, who still demand the converts' allegiance. Who, Paul asks, is your king now—Nero, the son of the dead-but-deified Emperor Claudius, or Jesus, the Son of the ever-living God? Are you going to fit what you can of Jesus' commands into the life that Nero expects of you, and no more? Or are you going to fit what you can of what Nero and this world's order expects of you into the life that Jesus calls you to lead, and no more?

Paul sees only two options: a person lives under the authority of darkness or under the kingship of God's Son. In this regard, he challenges our notions—perhaps better, our *illusions*—about freedom and about not having any king. If you're not living under Christ's lordship, Paul would tell us, you're still not your *own* boss. You're living under the dominion of darkness (Col 1:13).

Your own flesh, with its impulses and cravings, is your boss. It drives you; you're not free. The society around you is your boss, telling you what to value, what to chase after, keeping you running in exactly the ruts it has dug out for you. And deep down underneath your consciousness, *death* is your boss. As you keep trying to run away from it, it too has you running exactly as and where it wants you to run.

* * *

The good news in Colossians is that God has invaded and overpowered the kingdom of the flesh, the world, and death. God has brought about the time anticipated in Daniel, when the kingdoms of this world would be handed over to "one like a son of man," and that "Son of Man" is Jesus. To all of us who had lived under—and, indeed, been faithful subjects of—the flesh, the world, and death, God grants amnesty:

> In Christ we have redemption, the forgiveness of sins. (Col 1:14)

> Through Christ God was pleased to reconcile to himself all things, whether on earth or in heaven, by making peace through the blood of his cross. (Col 1:20)

He says in Christ, "Look! Bygones are bygones. Everything you've done to resist my reign up to this point is forgiven. The slate is wiped clean. I've won the battle for your liberation; I'm reigning now through my son, Jesus. He's your king now, so give him the same allegiance and obedience you used to give to his enemies, your former masters."

This Sunday reminds us year after year that Jesus is not only our Savior, born to give us a life of freedom from sin, death, and judgment. He's also our King, risen to exercise his rule through us who are his people, his subjects. We naturally gravitate to the part of the good news that highlights freedom from the dominion of darkness, but we tend to chafe against the part of the good news about living under a new King, a new Master, a new Lord. But without this second part, we never actually *experience* freedom from the power of darkness.

The "dominion of darkness" has personal, spiritual, and political dimensions. The challenge for us is to recognize these dimensions in the midst of a society that has shaped us to think that many aspects of the "dominion of darkness" are all right, even *good*, even our God-given right. We come to recognize this more and more, quite naturally, as we submit ourselves more and more fully to the rule of the kingdom of God's beloved Son. What this submission looks like is quite simple: we do what he says, more and more.

*　*　*

Jesus seemed to have been into reality checks. His reality check for Christ the King Sunday comes from Luke 6:46: "Why are you calling me 'Lord' when you're not doing what I tell you?" Inherent in calling Jesus "Lord" is the acknowledgment of his authority specifically as authority *over me*, the authority to direct my actions. It may not be accidental that the very next paragraph in Luke's Gospel begins the story of the centurion's exchange with Jesus while the centurion was seeking healing for his favorite domestic slave. The centurion told Jesus that he didn't have to trouble himself to come all the way to his house; if he would just speak the word from a distance, the centurion said, "I know my servant will be healed." The officer explained, and I paraphrase: "I understand authority and how authority works, because I'm *under* authority myself and I've got people under *my* authority. I tell one soldier to jump and he jumps; I tell another to drop and give me twenty, and he drops and gives me twenty." The centurion understood that Jesus had authority to command, and it would be so.

The question for us on this Christ the King Sunday is: Do *we* understand authority? Do *we* understand what it means to live under Jesus' authority—to call him "Lord" and live like we mean it because he says to do something and we do it? Do we make his kingship real in the little spheres of our lives, allowing him fully to annex us for his empire? Do we trust Jesus enough to believe that building our lives on his instructions makes for the securest existence we can enjoy?

> I will show you what someone is like who comes to me, hears my words, and acts on them. That one is like a man building a house, who dug deeply and laid the foundation on rock; when a flood arose, the river burst against that house but could not shake it, because it had been well built. But the one who hears and does not act is like a man who built a house on the ground without a foundation. When the river burst against it, immediately it fell, and great was the ruin of that house. (Luke 6:47–49 NRSV)

You don't have to be a spiritual mystic to hear Jesus' words; you just have to be able to read. And an obvious place to start reading is the four Gospels. Many modern publishers make our task even easier by printing Jesus' words in red. They practically jump off the page at us. I'm going to leave aside the whole somewhat bloated scholarly debate about how many such words actually go back to the historical Jesus. The important point is that we know a *lot* about what our King wants without having to wait for a special revelation from him.

Christ's kingship is inherent in God's plan for creation: "All things have been created *through* him and *for* him" (Col 1:16).

We get the first preposition: "All things have been created *through* him." As John wrote in the beginning of his Gospel, "In the beginning was the Word," and "all things came into being through him," and so forth. Do we really get the second: "All things were created *for* him"? People often seem to enjoy speculating: Why am I here? Why was I made? What is the purpose of this life? Paul thinks that he knows the answer, and it's embarrassingly simple. We were made through Christ, *for* Christ. We were made to bear witness to the rule of our King in this life by doing what he says. There is a purpose for our lives—it is to live as he tells us, to allow Christ to accomplish his purposes through us, to establish his kingdom in the space of what used to be our little fiefdoms.

God's purpose for the Son was "that he might come to have first place in all things" (Col 1:18). In *all* things? Does Jesus even have first place *here*? Does he have first place in *your* life? In *mine*? Does he have first place in this church? If we want to be genuine Christ-followers, and if we want our congregation truly to be a witness to Christ in this community, Paul raises these simple questions for us to keep before our eyes and in our conversations as a check on our plans, investments, and activities. Stop yourself every now and then throughout the day and develop the habit of asking yourself, "Is what I am doing, what I am speaking, what I am thinking reflecting Christ's holding first place in my life?" Let's stop ourselves every now and then when we're gathered in committee meetings, in church activities, in other events together, and ask each other, "Is this conversation, is the heart that each of us is bringing to this conversation, are the questions that we're asking and the plans that we're forming reflecting that Christ has preeminence—first place—in our gathering?"

Paul uses the image of the "head" and the "body" to put Christ in his proper place, and us in ours: "He is the head of the body, the church" (Col 1:18). What do we think about parts of a body that are nonresponsive—or even disobedient—to the directions coming from the head? We consider such parts spasmodic, diseased, malfunctioning, even dead. Think about your own body, over which you are the "head," the great "I," the "ego" that indwells and commands and moves your limbs in (ideally) whatever way you wish so as to accomplish what you wish. This is Paul's image for the universal church, except that no one of us is an "I" anymore. Christ is the "I," the ego, who defines and directs the motions of the whole body and each of its parts so as to accomplish what *he* wants. What Paul says of his own experience, he hopes all disciples will come to say: "It is no longer I who live, but Christ lives in me; the life I now live in the body I live by faith in the Son of God who loved me and gave himself for me" (Gal 2:20–21). I return frequently to this verse because it is so splendid an expression of the disciple who has arrived at God's goal for him or her.

There is a splendid reciprocity involved here. Paul only has to hint at it, because everyone living around the Mediterranean understands the importance of reciprocity, of responding appropriately to gifts or assistance given. "Through Jesus, God was pleased to reconcile to himself all things, whether on earth or in heaven, by making peace through the blood of his cross" (Col 1:20). We give ourselves to be the body of the one who "reconciled us in the body of his flesh," giving up that body on our behalf when we were still estranged from God. Is the part of the body that *you* represent as a disciple responsive to Jesus? Is the part of the body that *we* represent together as a community of disciples responsive?

* * *

Christ the King Sunday signals that we're approaching Advent. Like Lent, Advent is a wonderful time to increase our attention to our spiritual formation and maturation. For one thing, we're all kind of in a religious mood anyway, because it's almost the Christmas season and there are visual and auditory reminders of God and his Son everywhere. Advent is also an easier time than Lent for ramping up old spiritual disciplines or trying out new formational practices, since it's really short—just four weeks, three weeks shorter than Lent. So it's not as heavy a commitment.

If I hear from Jesus, I don't want it to be "Why are you calling me 'Lord, Lord,' but not doing what I say?" I imagine that none of us wants to be in a position to hear this. So I might suggest an Advent discipline such as the following. The terrible truth about discipleship is that it's like exercise: if you only attend to it once each week, you're not going to get anywhere with it. A sermon can't change you; only what you *do* with a sermon can move you on toward maturity in Christ.

So this is what I am suggesting for each of us this Advent. Spend some time each day reading and praying through the words of Jesus as collected either in Matthew or Luke. As you read and reflect on a single passage, paragraph, or even a single saying, ask yourself two simple questions: (1) What is Jesus really after when he says this or teaches that? and (2) How closely have I been lining up in my thoughts, words, and actions with what Jesus seems to be looking for? Ask Jesus for clear insight into your life and for clear direction about how to live out what he says more fully. Get yourself a little notebook for this exercise, and write down what you learn from the exercise each and every day. And if you're really up for a challenge, do this exercise with two or three other Christians with whom you can be open and to whom you can speak honestly. Another unfortunate rule of our culture is that we should keep religion a private matter; in the kingdom of God's Son, however, it is not so. Religion and our growth as disciples are very much collective matters. And it's the cyber age—you can do this through email or group messaging or video chat to make it easier. If, by the time Christmas rolls around, this exercise hasn't made a noticeable difference in your discipleship and witness, by all means *stop*.

Most of us are very familiar with the Great Commission that closes Matthew's Gospel: "Go therefore and make disciples of every nation, by baptizing them in the name of the Father and the Son and the Holy Spirit" (Matt 28:19). How many of us know what comes next? "And by teaching them to observe *all* things whatsoever that I have commanded you" (Matt 28:20). As we keep inviting people into a life of discipleship, let's be sure that we, too, keep becoming genuine disciples who *do* what our Lord *says*.

PART TWO

Sermons for Ordinary Time

21

"God's Bottom-Line Performance Metrics"

Galatians 5:16–25

Metrics. Every organization, it seems, has them now. I'm not talking about kilometers, kilograms, liters, and degrees centigrade. We tried all that here in America in the late 1970s, and it never really caught on. No, I'm talking about the numbers that fill in the blanks of reports, the numbers that are used to assess performance, effectiveness, profitability, and other indicators of corporate functioning. Even my school, Ashland Theological Seminary, in compliance with the Department of Education, has gone far in the direction of creating metrics. We come up with percentages of students attaining this or that learning outcome, with measurements of student satisfaction, with measurements of graduation and employment rates, all for the sake of giving a snapshot of our performance to accrediting agencies and proving that we are doing *some* kind of assessment to ensure the quality and effectiveness of our educational programs.

October is the month in which many United Methodist churches hold their "charge conferences," and those who prepare the reports for these meetings, which are then submitted to the district office and eventually trickle into the annual conference database, know how important metrics are in our denomination. We list average attendances, annual giving, percentages of apportionments met, numbers of new members, numbers of baptisms, average weekly participation in a variety of ministries, and so forth. These measurements—these metrics—provide hard data for assessing the performance and effectiveness of a given congregation.

But they don't touch on (in any direct way at least) another set of measurements, metrics, that seem to matter even more for how *God* would assess the performance and effectiveness of a congregation and of each of that congregation's individual disciples. Paul gives us one expression of these divine metrics in our passage from Galatians:

> Make it a habit to walk by the Spirit, and you will certainly not fulfill what the flesh desires. For the flesh yearns against what the Spirit desires, and the Spirit against what the flesh desires, for these stand opposed to one another in order that you may not do whatever you might want. But if you are being led by the Spirit, you are not under Torah. And the works born of the flesh are clearly evident: sexual immorality, impurity, shameless debauchery, idolatry, drug-induced spells, displays of enmity, strife, fanaticism, angry outbursts, self-promoting acts, dissensions, factions, acts born of envy, drunken bouts, gluttonous parties, and other things like these. Concerning these things I tell you in advance, just as I warned you before: those who keep on practicing such things will not inherit the kingdom of God.
>
> But the fruit produced by the Spirit is love, joy, peace, patience, kindness, goodness, faithfulness, forbearance, self-control. Against such things there is no law. And

those who are Christ's own crucified the flesh along with
its passions and desires. If we live by the Spirit, let us also
keep falling in step with the Spirit. (Gal 5:16–25)

What is of paramount importance to God—so Paul seems
to think—is whether our behavior, in private and in public, in
our homes and congregations and workplaces, shows that the
"flesh" is driving us or that the "Spirit" is driving us, that we are
giving mastery of ourselves over to the "flesh" or to the "Spirit."

I suggest that these metrics are more important than
the numerical ones that we will fixate on in preparation for
the charge conference. The *United Methodist Book of Discipline*
announces no penalties or promises for congregations that find
themselves on one or the other side of the conference's measurements like the ones we hear about from Paul in Galatians.
With regard to the outcomes of flesh-driven behavior, Paul
warns: "Concerning these things I tell you in advance, just as I
warned you before: those who keep on practicing such things
will not inherit the kingdom of God" (Gal 5:21). With regard
to both flesh-driven and Spirit-driven practice, Paul asserts:
"The harvest for those who continue to sow to their flesh will be
the rottenness of the grave, but for those who continue to sow
to the Spirit, the harvest will be eternal life" (Gal 6:8).

*   *   *

By "flesh," Paul does not mean the meat that clings to our bones.
Paul uses this word to name the bundle of self-centered, self-
serving impulses and drives that keep us falling short of God's
vision for us as God's new creation—God's vision for us as individuals and as a community of faith. The flesh is the "old person,"
the person we once were, the person from whom Christ died to
save us, reasserting itself, trying to stop the new creation from

coming about in us because that new creation means the death of the old creature. It is the Ego with a capital "E," trying to establish itself again on the throne of our lives because it doesn't want to be denied and it doesn't want to die. And Paul gives us clear metrics here. We know that the flesh is driving us—and that we are sowing to the flesh—when we see its works in us and among us. And these works are, as Paul says, obvious indeed when they show up: "sexual immorality, impurity, shameless debauchery, idolatry, drug-induced spells, displays of enmity, strife, fanaticism, angry outbursts, self-promoting acts, dissensions, factions, acts born of envy, drunken bouts, gluttonous parties, and other things like these."

I've been a part of this congregation long enough to know that not many of you are party animals, such that you *tend* not to manifest "drunken bouts" or "gluttonous parties." But we are hardly free from strife, dissension, angry outbursts, trying to get our own way, and getting in a tiff when we don't. We're not entirely free of sexual immorality and, statistics alone would tell us, of an array of addictions. These—and all such things—are warning signs to us, whether in our lives individually or in our life together, that we are sowing to the flesh—and are making ourselves once again liable to its harvest, the rottenness of the grave. Because if we're going to keep choosing to live the life of the old person, the unredeemed person, that's where we will end up and where all that is *us* will end.

The alternative to dredging up these flesh-driven works is to keep handing ourselves over to the Spirit, to become soil that is continuously cultivated by the Spirit such that the Spirit can produce its fruit in and among us. By "Spirit," Paul is not talking about our rational or better self, but the Holy Other who is wholly other—the Spirit of God, the Spirit of God's Son, who has invaded us in our baptism and seeks to pervade us in every situation, so that we are both driven and empowered by this Spirit to do and to become what is righteous and beautiful in God's sight.

The Spirit is too often treated as the third wheel in the Trinity. When we say the Apostles' Creed, we recite four lines about the Father, nine or ten lines about the Son, and *one* line about the Spirit. This doesn't begin to reflect the Holy Spirit's importance. Let's just consider what Paul has to say about the Spirit in the one short letter from which today's reading comes.

> Christ redeemed us from the curse pronounced by the law by becoming accursed on our behalf ... in order that the promise God made to Abraham might come to the nations in Christ Jesus—that is, in order that we might receive the promised Spirit by faith. (Gal 3:13–14)

> Because you are sons and daughters, God sent the Spirit of his Son into our hearts, crying "Abba, Father!" The result is that you're no longer a slave, but a child. (Gal 4:6–7)

> By means of the Spirit and on the basis of trusting, we are eagerly looking for the righteousness for which we hope. (Gal 5:5)

Paul seems to think that Christ died, among other goals, specifically to secure for us *this* promised gift—the Holy Spirit—to dwell within and among us. Paul seems to think that, if we have any sense at all that God has loved us and taken us into God's own family, this is the work of that same Spirit within us, assuring us and allowing us to call upon God as Father. Paul also seems to think that this gift of the Spirit is intended to get us from where we started out in our self-centered, self-serving unrighteousness to that place of being righteous, that place in which we hope to be found at the end of this journey when we stand before the God and Judge of all.

If I have one prayer for this congregation and each person in it, it is this: that each one of us, and all of us together, will grow in the fellowship of the Holy Spirit—the sensitivity to being aware of the Spirit's presence, the ability to know the Spirit's restraint and the Spirit's incitement, the discipline to get in step with the Spirit more and more.

Paul introduces today's reading with a marvelous promise: "Keep walking in line with and in the power of the Spirit, and *there's no way* that you'll bring what the flesh craves into being" (Gal 5:16). Christ did not die on our behalf to leave us caught between two opposite but equal powers, to be torn and continue to vacillate between the two. Christ died on our behalf to gain for us that divine power that could break the hold of the flesh over us and over our interactions together. God has put it within our grasp to live out there—and to live with one another in here, even in our committee meetings!—in such a manner as consistently manifests the fruit of the Spirit, such that we continue to allow God to clothe us with love, joy, peaceful relationships, patience, generosity toward others, goodness, steadfast reliability, forbearance, and self-control. If we all together seek the leading of the Holy Spirit for whatever ministry, committee, or group of which we are a part here—the leading of the Holy Spirit, not the leading of our own inner sense of what needs to happen and our frustration, then impatience, then anger with the other people here who get in our way—the outcome must be that we will proceed in all things together harmoniously.

*   *   *

What is required of us to attain this? First, I suppose, we have to buy into Paul's metrics and into his claim that God cares, perhaps first and foremost, whether we are taking hold of the new life his Spirit makes possible or continuing to indulge our old person in spite of Christ's death to save us from that person and its destiny. Second, we need to commit ourselves—daily, even hourly—to "keep walking in line with the Spirit," to maintain vigilance over our own impulses so that, when we recognize the impulses of the flesh, we can turn immediately to the Spirit for timely help and power to squelch those impulses and fall in step instead with the Spirit's better direction. In this manner, it requires diligent and disciplined dying—identifying, denying, and dying to those self-centered drives, those self-protective impulses, those flesh-feeding urges that keep churning up the mucky works of the flesh. Conversely, it requires regularly reorienting ourselves so that we seek the Spirit's leading in situation after situation until the Spirit-born impulses become our *first* impulses.

Epictetus was born around the same time that Paul wrote Galatians. He was born a slave but became one of the most influential Stoic philosophers of the Roman period. He taught those who wanted to attain the Stoic ideal—inner freedom from external stimuli that allowed them to remain in control of themselves, possessed of virtue, and unperturbed in mind—that this was possible if they would just train themselves to keep that goal ever before them.

> When you go into the market, don't think only that you want to get the good fish or vegetables before they're gone, but also that you want to remain possessed of virtue. When you go into the council chamber, don't think only that you want to persuade the council to vote one

way or another, but also that you want to maintain your
self-control. When you go to the public baths, don't think
only that you want to enjoy a restful time and get a good
massage, but also that you want to remain unperturbed
in mind. That way, when you get to the market and rude
people push in ahead of you or grab the choice fish out
from under you, you will not be dragged into becoming
rude yourself, but will remember—"I didn't just come
here to get fish or vegetables, but to keep my virtue
intact." When you get into the council chamber and angry
men oppose your proposal and call you foolish, you won't
get riled up to respond in kind, but will remember—"I
didn't just come here to win a debate, but also to maintain
my self-control." When you get to the bathhouse and a
rowdier bunch spoils your rest with splashing and rau-
cous banter, you will remember—"I didn't just come here
for a restful massage, but also to remain unperturbed in
mind." The first of each pair of goals is always vulnerable
to being foiled; the second goal of each pair is in no one's
power to foil but your own.[1]

We can learn a lot from Epictetus's advice, with this important change: our second goal, really our underlying and indispensable goal, in every situation is this—that we will keep in
step with the Spirit in every situation and not give ourselves
over to what the flesh might impel us to do. I would urge us to
be especially attentive to this in our work, our activities, our
ministries together as a congregation. The ugly stereotype of a
church these days is that it is a place marked by "displays of
enmity, strife, angry outbursts, self-promoting acts, dissensions,

1. This is my paraphrase of Epictetus, *Enchiridion* 4.

factions"—all flesh-driven works. Let's be vigilant to banish all of these from every corner of our church by giving none of them so much as a corner within ourselves. The beauty of the alternative is irresistible—a community characterized by "love, joy, peace, patience, kindness, goodness, faithfulness, forbearance, self-control"—a Spirit-shaped culture. These are God's metrics, and he has supplied us, in his Spirit, with all that we need to measure up.

22

"Jesus Christ, Investment Planner"

Luke 12:13–21, 32–34; 2 Corinthians 9:6–15

W e're looking at a crowded restaurant, listening to the din of conversations rising up from every table. We happen to catch one distinct line from one of the tables: "Well, my broker is E. F. Hutton, and E. F. Hutton says ..." And suddenly the room falls into complete silence. No one is interested in their own conversations any more so much as interested to hear what tip will be reported as having fallen from the lips of E. F. Hutton.

What about when Jesus speaks about investment strategies? Do we believe that we're about to hear a profoundly profitable tip from *him*?

> Don't be afraid, little flock, because your Father is very happy to give you the kingdom. Sell your possessions and give to those in need; provide money bags for yourself that won't wear out, an inexhaustible treasure in the heavens where a thief doesn't encroach and a moth-worm doesn't devour. For where your treasure is, there your heart will also be. (Luke 12:32–34)

The investment strategies of our commercial banking industry and our capitalist economy are all about laying up for ourselves treasure on earth. Every investment planner with a shingle out there will help you lay up your treasure on earth wisely, to diversify your portfolio so as to achieve the right balance of risk and return for your stage of life with a view to preserving capital while gaining sufficient dividends and income to keep you in the lifestyle to which you've become accustomed. Of course we need enough to raise our families and get our children launched; of course we need enough to remain self-sufficient to the extent possible. But let's be honest. We—especially here in America—have a problem defining "enough." There are strong forces at work all around us trying to make excess seem insufficient and leave us wanting even more.

That's where we find the "hero" of Jesus' parable. He's a landowner who has apparently managed his estate well and whose crops have yielded abundant returns over the years. He gets to the point where the storage facilities that he once built, anticipating that they would be big enough, aren't big enough for all his assets anymore. His response is to build even bigger storage bins to store the excess and to think only of how great the rest of *his* life is going to be, with all those assets upon which to draw. It actually sounds enviable. Indeed, it has the makings of a good slogan for an investment company—"Gulf Shores Capital Investments. *You're* going to need bigger barns." But then God shows up, and the man's real poverty is exposed. "You did very well for yourself. You were living the dream. But now that's all over and you're standing before me. What do you have now?"

A lot of Christians hear Scriptures like these begrudgingly as if Jesus is trying to make us make ourselves poorer. But that's not the case at all. Jesus is trying to teach us how to make ourselves *richer*, and to make ourselves richer *forever*. There *is* wealth that

we *can* take with us. The trick is that we have to make this kind
of wealth before we go. We have to believe enough in forever to
invest for forever.

*   *   *

There is a wonderfully edifying second-century Christian text
that almost nobody reads anymore. It's called the *Shepherd of
Hermas* and, among other things, it contains what is perhaps our
earliest surviving homily on the Gospel lesson we read today.

> You know that you who are servants of God are living
> in a foreign country, for *your* city is far from *this* city. If,
> then, you know in what city you are destined to live, why
> are you furnishing for yourselves plots of land and piles
> of stuff and buildings and empty rooms *here*? ... So exer-
> cise prudence. As a person residing in a foreign country,
> do not furnish yourself with *one thing more* than is neces-
> sary to be self-sufficient. Instead of buying acreage here,
> ransom lives that are in distress; look after the vulnerable
> and don't neglect them. Spend your wealth and posses-
> sions, which you've received from God anyway, on goods
> of *this* kind, which you will find in your own city when you
> go home to it. ... Don't practice the same kind of extrav-
> agant spending as the unbelievers, but practice your
> distinctive kind of extravagance, which will bring you
> joy forever.[1]

The people whose lives we have touched for the better, personally or from a great distance, constitute our treasure in
heaven. The people whose lives we have rescued from or supported in the midst of distress, whose hearts have been opened

1. *Similitude* 1, my paraphrase.

to God and God's salvation by our outreach, whose needs we have shouldered as our own so as to help them carry their burdens—we will find these people again on the other side of death, and the love that we expressed for them here, the relief that we brought them here, the spiritual nurture and growth that we facilitated for them here will make of them our treasure in heaven forever.

So Jesus is calling us into his brokerage office this morning and wants to ask of us: Do you need to diversify your investment portfolio? Are you positioned too strongly in short-term investments—that is to say, investments that will pay off on *this* side of death? Have you taken adequate thought for your long-term needs and invested accordingly so that you can enjoy a rich lifestyle for the eternity on the other side of death? Is some reallocation of assets in order?

Jesus keeps calling our attention to good investment opportunities, inviting us to invest in the kingdom of God, to get behind ventures that seek to facilitate the kingdom's breaking in and becoming real here, in *this* world, so that when we leave this country in which we are merely sojourners and resident aliens, and enter our eternal homeland, we will find and enjoy the fruits of those assets we have invested in the kingdom, the rewards of the time and labor we have committed to the kingdom, the well-deserved rest that follows the energies we have expended for the kingdom.

Of course I'm speaking, in part at least, about the ministries of the local church and our support of the same with, as our membership vows put it, "our prayers, our presence, our gifts, and our service."[2] And I'm talking *this* morning, without embarrassment, chiefly about our gifts. Supporting the ministries of

2. *The United Methodist Hymnal* (Nashville: Abingdon Press, 1989), 38.

the church is one instrument in a solid investment strategy for eternity. We offer a somewhat diversified portfolio here—we're a kind of "balanced assets" mutual fund for the kingdom.

You're investing in your own growth as a disciple and in the growth that we are all potentially experiencing here together. What you give makes it possible also for *others* to experience (hopefully) well-crafted and impactful worship, education in the faith, meaningful connections with other Christians that create a network of holy and loving support for your *own* perseverance in faith to the end. You invest in the faith formation of our children and youth, whose lives have the potential to be set on a strong foundation for this life and for eternity because of this work. You invest in the work of missionaries in foreign lands, in the kingdom fruit of whose missions you have a share. You engage in missions and relief efforts yourself and support the mission and relief work of others. You invest in the much larger mission of the United Methodist Church globally through our church's apportionments, which, while of course supporting the denomination's administrative structures, also support the positive kingdom work of those structures as well as a variety of denominational outreach and relief efforts. And we *do* need to make sure that everything given to support this church is responsibly used to create kingdom dividends. When we're not, we expect you, the shareholders, to point out those areas where an audit is in order with a view to maximizing kingdom impact.

But I'm not just talking about investing *here* in the life of our local church. As I said, we're a good balanced-assets kingdom fund. But you might also need some good kingdom growth funds in your ERA—your "eternal retirement account." Are there frontline ministries toward which God would direct your attention and some part of the resources that he's entrusted to you? Perhaps those specialized organizations that seek to bring resources and aid to persecuted Christians and the surviving families of martyrs throughout Asia and Africa so that they know the support, love, and encouragement of the global family of God and can persevere in their costly witness? Perhaps those organizations dedicated to making the Scriptures freely available to people throughout the world in their own languages, so that the Holy Spirit can do in their lives what the Spirit does in ours when we engage God's word? Perhaps those relief agencies that work diligently and responsibly to secure a sustainable life for entire villages or to provide timely relief from starvation or disease? Perhaps those ministries that work with at-risk youth in our cities or nurture faith and discipleship on college campuses? Perhaps scholarship funds that support the training of a new generation of pastors, missionaries, and theological educators?

You might also consider if you should invest in some individual kingdom stocks for your portfolio as well. Is there a single-parent family that could stand to be informally adopted, both for the relief of a working parent and for the care, nurture, and sound guidance of his or her children? Is there a particular Christian family or community in an underresourced or even hostile area of the globe with which you are called to partner?

Our second-century pastor urges us: "Spend your wealth and possessions, which you've received from God anyway, on goods of *this* kind, which you will find in your own city when you go home to it. ... Don't practice the same kind of extravagant spending as the unbelievers, but practice your distinctive kind of extravagance, which will bring you joy forever." Rightly interpreting Jesus' advice, he calls us to invest adequately in people, with whom our relationships will therefore outlast our deaths, whom we will enjoy forever in the communion of saints. Ultimately, we are talking about genuinely and

fully loving our neighbors as ourselves and doing so with a view
to accomplishing in their lives what God deeply wishes to see
accomplished—or even to accomplishing in God's name what
they themselves are praying to God to accomplish for them.

*   *   *

As we leave Jesus' brokerage firm, his receptionist Paul throws
two good words our way. First, he says, remember this: "The
one who throws only a little into these investments will only
enjoy a small return, but the one who invests heavily in these
ventures will have a whopping return. But you can invest whatever you decide to invest—it's up to you; no one's putting a gun
to your head. For God loves the cheerful investor" (2 Cor 9:6–7).[3]
In some stewardship campaigns, I've heard people talk about
tithing, asserting that, according to the Scriptures, 10 percent
of our income belongs to God, pushing the congregation to keep
bumping up their giving closer to 10 percent. It would be fabulous to see this congregation tithe. This church would be flush
with funds and would have to begin seriously considering what
new outreaches and ministries we would need to add, what new
missionaries we would need to support, what new relief efforts
we would need to undertake in order to spend the income. The
expenses of running this place would not increase; only our
ability to have a kingdom impact would increase.

But I don't see Jesus or Paul in these texts pushing us to tithe.
I've simply heard both, in different ways, asking us if we're using
our temporary wealth intelligently with a view to what will
make us rich before God, what will accrue eternal dividends,
because those dividends will be with us forever. I see both of
them simply holding out an investment opportunity before us,

---

3.   I'm admittedly taking liberties with this rendering.

urging us to make the most of it. The unavoidable flip side of this is that if we don't seriously consider these investment opportunities, we will, in some fashion that we cannot envision precisely but that should nevertheless give us pause, be without those dividends forever. I personally trust the Holy Spirit and each one of you to work out the right level of investment and how the whole portfolio needs to be put together to maximize your kingdom impact.

A second thing Paul shoots at us on our way out is this: "God is able to make all favor abound to you in order that, having enough for your needs, you may abound in every good work" (2 Cor 9:8). Paul makes us ask: Does God bring resources our way to bless *us* (so that we enjoy its *temporary* benefits) or to empower us to bless *others* (so that we enjoy its *eternal* benefits)?

There's yet another layer to this. The financial resources that we're talking about have value to us only as long as we are alive or this world lasts, but God has made it possible for us to use this money now, before it becomes valueless, to purchase what will be of eternal value to us. If you know that a particular government is going down, does it make better sense to hold on to its currency or work out some exchange before it's too late? You may have heard the exclamation, "Hold on to your Confederate money! The South will rise again!" No, I think those people who started exchanging their Confederate money in 1863 or 1864 for commodities that would still have value on the other side of the Confederacy's fall were the wise ones. And Jesus doesn't want us to find ourselves standing before him at the last judgment essentially holding bags of Confederate money. He wants us surrounded by the commodities of eternal value for which we've exchanged the currency of this world and its kingdoms.

When you get to heaven—and I'm not talking about buying or earning your way in, but Jesus' language should make us think about what it's going to be like for us on the other side of getting in—do you want to be surrounded by all the good you haven't done? For eternity? Or will you want to be surrounded by all the good to which you have contributed—in which you have invested—as fully as possible? Maybe when Jesus, our investment planner, speaks, we should listen.

23

"From Consumers to Producers"

Ephesians 4:1–16

You need only open your Sunday newspaper to know that we live in a consumer economy. Drop it on the floor, and sixteen flyers for various stores touting their sales or packets of coupons and special offers will go flying across the tiles. In fact, we're so much a consumer economy that I would bet that a lot of us like to get the Sunday paper specifically for those inserts (and the comics, of course). Our consumer culture has trained us pretty well, and it generally has all of Sunday afternoon through the following Saturday night to train and retrain us to be consumers of goods and services. It keeps trying to get us to look at everything in terms of what we can get out of it, what it will do for us, such that we should give it our attention and our business.

We believe that we should be able to get just about anything we want, whenever we want it, at the lowest prices out there—and we generally *can*, which only reinforces these convictions. We expect to walk into a store or restaurant and to be given a high level of courteous, friendly service (whether or not the salesperson or the server has a sick child at home who's been vomiting all night, is preoccupied with a parent with dementia, or sees the handwriting on the wall that his or her marriage is over). We expect the restaurant to look just the way it did when we were last there—because we liked it that way—and to be playing the music that we expect to hear there—because we like it that way. If the server forgot to have the chef hold the onions in the salad, we're disappointed and might put less into the tip. And let's not even get into the whole entertainment industry and its pandering to every taste and preference.

The single best representation for the mindset that our consumer economy and culture deliberately seek to nurture in us comes to us from Burger King: "Have it your way." This is the motto that has shaped our consumerist credo: "I believe that I should be able to have it, whatever 'it' is, and to have it *my* way, just the way *I* like it."

And, perhaps, that creed is generally appropriate *out there*. I choose to frequent certain restaurants because I know that I'll be able to carry on a conversation without having to shout or strain to listen over the music. If those restaurants change the ambiance, I will eat somewhere else. If the breadsticks come out cold and a bit hard, I'm going to ask for fresh ones instead. The restaurant owner and I have a shared vision and set of values *out there*, one in which satisfying customer expectations, within reason, is a core value. The problem arises—and indeed, this problem has become epidemic—when we bring this mindset back with us into the church of Christ.

We bump into this mindset whenever we evaluate our experience at church on the basis of our own satisfaction or dissatisfaction, whether our assessment is positive ("I get a lot out of that service"; "That class really meets my needs") or negative ("I don't get much out of his sermons"; "I don't like it when they serve Communion *that* way"; "I wish they'd do the hymns *I* like").

We bump into this mindset when we find ourselves expecting the paid staff to always give us service with a smile, when we're impatient with changes to the décor (because it's not the way *I* like it), or when we didn't get the goods or services we felt entitled to receive ("I was in the hospital for a colonoscopy and the pastor didn't come to see me").

Brothers and sisters, the church of Jesus Christ is *not* Burger King. If you come here to "have it your way," you're largely missing the point of coming here in the first place, which is to learn how to deny ourselves, shoulder up the cross that Jesus shouldered, and follow him who prayed in Gethsemane, "I don't have to have it *my* way; let it be done *your* way."

*   *   *

So what alternative vision does God hold out for his church? Paul's letter to the Christians in Ephesus, from beginning to end, provides a virtual manifesto of this alternative vision, and I commend the reading of the whole to you at some point. The passage before us today in particular lays out this vision for our life and work together as a congregation.

The first challenge that Paul directs to us is to approach one another in a spirit that is productive of unity and harmony within the household of God, within the body of Christ—to be *producers of unity*.

> I therefore, the prisoner in the Lord, beg you to lead a life worthy of the calling to which you have been called, with all humility and gentleness, with patience, bearing with one another in love, making every effort to maintain the unity of the Spirit in the bond of peace. There is one body and one Spirit, just as you were called to the one hope of your calling, one Lord, one faith, one baptism, one God

and Father of all, who is above all and through all and in
all. (Eph 4:1-6 nrsv)

If you track down almost everyone who has grumbled in the
church, everyone who has led a covert crusade against someone
else in the church, everyone who has *left* a church, in the majority of cases it comes down to this: "I didn't have it my way." That
consumerist mentality works well to keep stores competitive
and service adequate, but it is corrosive to the body of Christ.
Now please don't misunderstand me. I'm not talking about
disagreement and discussion—the first is unavoidable and
the second is necessary. I'm talking about the disgruntlement, the
discord, and the dislike that all too often follow when the discussion or disagreement doesn't go our way.

We have been called to a different mindset and a different goal: to commit ourselves to one another and to make it
our highest priority to maintain that uniting bond by adopt-
ing a humble and gentle spirit toward one another, by showing
patience toward one another, by putting up with one another
because we are all a part of each other. We have, all of us, been
immersed into *one* baptism that made all of us together the *one*
body that Christ has pervaded with the *one* Holy Spirit. We all
stand together before *one* Lord, united by *one* hope—to become
citizens forever (and, for the record, stuck with one another
forever) in the kingdom of God. We are united by *one* faith into
a single family by virtue of calling upon *one* God as the Father
of us all. Is there not enough in all these *ones* to motivate us to
hold on to one another in love? Are these *ones* of less value than
the superficial details over which we feed dissatisfaction and
eventually division? If we come with the consumer mentality,
disunity and division will be inevitable, because all of the details
will not ever be to everyone's preferences and tastes; we simply

cannot *all* have it our way. In sum, then, we are called by God to stop being *consumers* focused on getting what we want, the way we want it, and to commit ourselves fully to being *producers of unity* within this portion of the body of Christ. Only if we do that are we living in a manner worthy of Christians, worthy of our calling.

*   *   *

The second challenge of Paul's vision for the church is for each and every one of us to move away from being simply a consumer of what ministries provide toward becoming *producers of ministry* together. It is not for the parishioner to ask the church, "What have you done for me lately?" It is for Christ to ask each one of us and all of us together, "What have you done for *me* lately?" And it is perfectly just for him to ask this of us, for he gave his body to be nailed up on the cross in order to bring us into this body together; he supplies us with his Spirit to empower us in ministry and with his pastors and teachers to equip us for ministry.

> But grace was given to each one of us according to Christ's measuring out of his gift. Therefore it says, "Ascending on high, he took captivity itself captive; he gave gifts to people." ... He himself gave apostles, prophets, evangelists, pastors and teachers, to equip the saints for the work of ministry, for building up the body of Christ, until we all attain to the oneness that comes from the faith and from knowing the Son of God—until we all attain to maturity, to measuring up to Christ's stature in all his fullness. (Eph 4:7-8, 11-13)

Paul indirectly but not too subtly calls himself God's gift to the church. He *is* an apostle, an evangelist, a pastor, and a teacher. But he also identifies the primary purpose of Christ's giving such figures to be "to equip the saints for the work of ministry—to equip the saints for the building up of the body of Christ."

I know that some Christians have a knee-jerk reaction to hearing the preacher try to lay the burden of the work of ministry upon the congregation. I can see a few thought bubbles, in fact: "That's what we're paying *you* for! You want *me* to do your job for you?" And I do have to admit that our church structures are different from Paul's. Among the thirty or so Christians that gathered in one of the more spacious houses of one of the wealthier Christians in Ephesus, there were no paid staff. If *any* work of ministry was going to happen, it was going to be because the Christians all took it upon themselves to do it. Paul's churches' situation was a far cry from what we have here—full-time pastor, church administrator, and custodian; part-time youth and children's ministry personnel, part-time communications and finance personnel, part-time music personnel; missionaries supported by our church financially. There is certainly a sense in which the majority of you are behind *all* the ministry that happens here insofar as you have committed to support a few particular Christians, enabling us to devote more of our time to advancing the mission of the church.

This does not, however, fundamentally alter the scriptural vision for the church; it does not rob you of the *privilege* nor relieve you of the *responsibility* of God's call to you to have a share in "the work of ministry, the building up of the body of Christ." Nor does it alter the primary scriptural mandate for the apostles, evangelists, pastors, and teachers that God raises up—to equip you, the saints, for the work of ministry.

I imagine that you're all accustomed to hearing the phrase "the building up of the body of Christ" and to thinking about it in one of its two key aspects—namely, the aspect of making one another's faith stronger, encouraging one another in times of difficulty, sharpening one another's understanding of discipleship, and the like. We might think of this as the fitness-center aspect of bodybuilding—our work together making those of us who are already here in the body stronger, more fit for living as disciples. This is indeed an important aspect, one that I would never wish to underplay.

For example, Stephen Ministry—as I know many of you are aware already—is an amazing example of a program that quite directly equips saints for the work of ministry, for the building up of the body of Christ, specifically for coming alongside its more distressed cells and facilitating God's repair of those cells. The person who goes through Stephen Ministry training will get a better foundation in the skills of Christian caregiving than a seminary student preparing for parish ministry, if that student only takes the typical required course in pastoral care. This is a marvelous opportunity for you to be equipped for a particular kind of work of ministry, and the skills you will learn here spill over into many other, briefer caring encounters that you could have both with fellow Christians *and* with people in your circles who are not yet incorporated into the body of Christ.

Which brings me to the other key aspect of "building up the body of Christ." Paul is actually using a construction site metaphor, not an exercise metaphor. His audience in Ephesus would also hear "the building up of the body of Christ" as "the ongoing construction of the body of Christ." It's admittedly a mixed metaphor, but it calls attention to all the blocks of stone out there that are still being fitted into a building under construction. The body of Christ itself is not yet complete. It is still under construction—not merely in the sense that you and I have some distance to go until we are complete in our individual or corporate discipleship, but also in the sense that there are yet parts of Christ's body out there, not yet connected to the body. Christ has not yet come to his fullness in this world because he has not yet fitted those people to be joined to his body, the church.

I would not choose between these key aspects but would rather see us throw ourselves into the work of both. We must put ourselves at God's disposal to use us to build one another up in the faith until we all reach maturity in Christ; we must put ourselves at God's disposal to use us to continue to construct and complete the as-yet-incomplete body of Christ, some of whose members are still out there, not yet incorporated into Christ's body, until the church has become "the complete person" (which is another way to translate the Greek that the NRSV renders "to maturity" in 4:13), the "complete person" that is the body of which Christ is the head.

Now, while Paul talks specifically about apostles, prophets, evangelists, pastors, and teachers as Christ's "gifts" to the church for the sake of equipping it to fulfill its calling, he first spoke more generally of "each one of us" as people to whom "grace was given according to the measure Christ set for his giving." He also speaks of each Christian as gifted in some way by God for the good of the whole body of Christ. God longs for each one of us to cease coming here with the mindset of looking to get something, which inevitably leads to becoming disgruntled when we don't get what we want or enough of what we want, and to come here consistently with the mindset of looking to *be* a gift to the other people here with us, to become consistently a medium through which God can touch other people's lives for growth, healing, restoration, encouragement. *You* are the means that God has chosen by which the Spirit will produce good for the whole.

* * *

The Spirit's goal is that we would all arrive together at maturity in Christ, that we would all live and speak and want and relate from that mind of Christ that was so full of God and the doing of God's good will that there will be no room left over for our being full of ourselves. The purpose is

> that we should no longer be children, tossed this way and that and blown about by every wind of doctrine, by people's trickery, by the wiles of their deceitful scheming. But, speaking the truth in love, let us grow in every way into him who is the head, into Christ, from whom the whole body, joined and knit together by every ligament with which it is equipped, as each part is working properly, promotes the body's growth in building itself up in love. (Eph 4:14–16)

Now, we are not much shaken and tossed about *here* by new winds of doctrine or by the wiles of deceivers, but many of us *are* shaken and tossed about—and thus the *church* experiences the turmoil of such tossing about—by frustrations and conflicts born of the consumerist mindset among churchgoers. Seneca, a philosopher who was Paul's contemporary, speaks of those "whose childishness persists long after their hair has turned gray,"[1] and I would not have that be true for anyone here. Paul's third challenge to us is to become *producers of maturity*—in ourselves, by growing in our connection to the living Jesus and habituating ourselves to putting ourselves out for the other person, serving Christ's agenda for our church rather than clamoring for what we want. We are called to be producers of

---

1. *On Firmness* 12.1 (my translation).

maturity in others by speaking to them, lovingly, the truth that they need to hear and keeping their eyes fixed on the *real* reasons we're all here together.

God's vision for the church is beautiful and amazing—a community of love so unlike the self-centered, self-gratifying, self-serving society around us that it shines like the brightest star in the blackest night. If we give ourselves fully over to this vision, not one of us need fear disappointment with the outcome.

24

"Faith Is Just the Beginning"

2 Peter 1:3–11; Mark 4:1–20

The winds were already exceeding gale force, blowing dead fronds and empty bins across yards and streets, causing palm trees to bend and sway like participants in an aerobics class. Sheets of rain were slapping the car as its driver strained through the overtaxed wipers to spot the next arrow pointing to the hurricane evacuation route. She finally saw one, pointing her to the right, then another telling her to continue straight, then another signaling her to turn left onto the northbound interstate. She pulled onto the entrance ramp, emerged on the broad space of the highway, pulled over to the shoulder, turned off her engine, and fell back into her seat. "Thank God! I made it!" she said, as she sat there, watching the other traffic press on by, wondering what their hurry was.

It's an admittedly ridiculous story. And yet, this is essentially how the author of 2 Peter would view the person who said that she got saved when she made a public confession of Jesus at a revival or church camp or altar call some twenty years ago but who hadn't traveled *any* distance up the highway toward Christlikeness, toward living for others, toward giving herself over more and more fully to allowing God to accomplish his purposes for who she would become and what fruit she would bear for him over the rest of the course of her life. For the author of 2 Peter, salvation isn't just a matter of an isolated decision. It's a matter of following an evacuation route. Decision is important, but it has to be a decision to follow the evacuation route, because salvation—safety—lies at the *end* of an evacuation route, not at its beginning.

John Wesley and the people called Methodists shared this author's view of salvation to a great extent. Among the early Methodists, the principal entrance requirement to the group was a "desire to flee from the wrath to come," and the nature of that flight was a lifelong commitment to use all the help that God had provided, all of "the means of grace," to grow in holiness and righteousness. The movement's members sought, and encouraged one another, to exercise all diligence in discovering how to withdraw themselves from doing any harm and how to invest themselves in doing all the good they could, all the while seeking that "second rest" that was believed to be the Holy Spirit's goal for each and every Christian—namely, arrival at that place where love for God and love for neighbor drove all of one's actions and interactions. Following Christ entailed a "long obedience in the same direction,"[1] not "a long inertia in the same pew."

Do you understand that you are still in the process of fleeing? Or have you stopped running away from the direction of what is harmful and in the direction of safety—of *salvation*—too soon?

*   *   *

---

1. A phrase found in Friedrich Nietzsche, *Beyond Good and Evil* 5.188, and appropriated by Eugene Peterson in his book of that name.

Our text begins its portrait of the Christian's life by talking not only about God's astounding gifting but also by giving some clear definition to the purposes behind God's gifting of those who came to acknowledge the Lord who was calling them:

> His divine power has given us all things with a view to life and piety through the acknowledgment of the One who called us by his own glory and virtue, through which he has given to us the precious and very great promises, in order that, through these, you might become participants in the divine nature, fleeing from the corruption that is in the world through desire. (2 Pet 1:3-4)

This is a portrait of a God who has invested heavily in us. The author shows us a God who has supplied us with all that we need to arrive at "life and piety," an expression that might be better taken to mean, in English, "a pious life" or "a life of godliness," a life reshaped with concern for God and for what is due God as the center and organizing principle of this new life. Our acknowledging Jesus as our Lord and Savior is indeed important here, as is our acknowledgment that we have been called and selected not on the basis of any merit or value that we brought to the table but rather on the basis of "his own glory and virtue"—because providing for us the way back to God's embrace and the way forward to the kingdom of God's Son seemed to God to be most in keeping with God's generous, noble, redemptive character. But, says Peter, God delivers us into that kingdom not by some instantaneous teleportation but rather by equipping us for pilgrimage, empowering us to make a long journey of obedience in the direction of that kingdom.

It is a journey of slogging through and leaving behind "the corruption"—the decay, the ruin, the rot—"that is in the world"—more to the point, that is in us, to the extent that we have been shaped by our society—"because of desire" (2 Pet 1:4). It's quite countercultural for me as an American to think about "desire" as something negative. I encounter all kinds of encouragement to "dream big" of enjoying the goods and pleasures of this life, even in terms of achieving great things as my society-shaped peers define them. I encounter all manner of enticements seeking to stimulate my desire, whether for a new appliance, a new car, a new medication, a new drink, a new snack, a new restaurant, a new beach resort, a new movie, a new computer, new kitchen cabinets, a new vehicle. Wanting seems to be as normal, as necessary, as breathing in the world that I know.

Our author speaks to us from a distant culture, one that knew just as well as we do what it was to desire but that was also more critical, more suspicious, when it came to desire and its effects on a human life. A commonplace of ethics throughout the Greek and Roman periods was this: in order to arrive at a consistently virtuous life, one's reason had always and consistently to maintain the upper hand over one's desires. To give free rein to one's impulses, desires, and feelings was to abandon the pursuit of the virtues that *made* a life worth living. Early Christian ethics would be no less rigorous.

Our author warns us that desire has contributed to the corruption of God's good world and God's good vision for life in this world in so many ways. Consider greed, which leads to ecologically unsustainable practices, to oppression of the weak so that the empowered can enjoy a larger share of coveted goods, to withholding other people's access to enough so that I can have access to more. Or consider sexual desire, which leads to the warping and breaking of relationships, even to systematic and often violent victimization of people who are transformed into objects of lust. But desire doesn't have to lead to such obvious evils to contribute to the corruption—the ruin—that is in the world. I suspect that, for most of us, the greatest threat comes from vanilla desires that simply distract us, occupy us, and siphon off our time, attention, and energy from pressing on along the evacuation route that God has laid out for us and for which God has equipped us, with the result that we run the risk of being found still puttering around uselessly at ground zero when the hurricane strikes.

But there is also *holy* desire. God has given us "precious and very great promises," and the author would only encourage us to desire these things. What would these promises include? Surely that we might become reflections of God's own righteousness in this world by the working of his Spirit within and among us; that we might be elevated to participate in the divine nature, sharing in God's virtue and goodness rather than this world's corruption; that we might be given lavish entrance into the eternal kingdom of our Lord Jesus Christ, a place in God's unfiltered presence forever. God's promises hold before us that which is indeed worth desiring. If we train our desires on what God has promised us, desire will work for us instead of against us; we will put aside being self-directed unto distraction at best and destruction at worst, and allow ourselves to be impelled in the direction of salvation.

* * *

The author lays out a path—an escape plan, an evacuation route—by which to keep putting the world that is subject to decay and ruin further behind us and to keep moving forward in the direction of the "entrance into the eternal kingdom of our Lord Jesus Christ" that shall mark our arrival in the safe, everlasting harbor.

> Bringing all diligence indeed to bear in respect of this
> very thing, supply, in your faith, virtue in addition; and
> in your virtue, knowledge; and in your knowledge, self-
> control; and in your self-control, endurance; and in your
> endurance, godliness; and in your godliness, love for the
> brothers and sisters; and in your love for the brothers
> and sisters, love without boundaries (*agapē*). For as
> these things belong to and abound among you, they will
> ensure that you are not unproductive or unfruitful in
> regard to your acknowledgment of our Lord Jesus Christ.
> (2 Pet 1:5–8)

"Bring all diligence to bear," the author says. "Make every effort; invest yourself in this path that God has opened up for you, and do so in such a manner and to such an extent that shows that you understand its value!"

Coming to faith is just the beginning, the starting point for this evacuation plan: "In the midst of your faith, provide yourself also with virtue." Reflect more and more the character of the Lord you have acknowledged.

In the midst of growing in virtue, provide yourself with knowledge. Keep learning; keep yourself in the word until the word has fully infiltrated *you*; keep exerting yourself to understand more and more fully the contours of the life to which Jesus has called you, the life for your living of which he handed over his own life!

In the midst of growing in knowledge, provide yourself with self-control—the natural and key quality to seek and attain in areas where desire is the principal source of the corruption, the decay, the ruin from which you are escaping.

In the midst of growing in self-control, provide yourself with endurance. Keep up the energy for this flight over the long haul, maintaining resistance in the face of every enticement and distraction, pushing back against the astounding cultural forces at work against our commitment to self-control—the forces daily preaching self-gratification, self-indulgence, self-centered investment.

In the midst of endurance, provide yourself with godliness, living a life that has God at its center, that places giving to God what is God's due as the highest priority.

In the midst of such God-centered living, cultivate a love for your sisters and brothers. Invest yourself in building up relationships of deep caring and mutual commitment among the family that God has called together and created by virtue of giving us all—all in the global church—new birth into God's own family, with Jesus as the firstborn of many sisters and brothers.

In the midst of loving your sisters and brothers, cultivate that love that knows no boundaries, the love that depends on nothing external, no kinship bond whether natural or spiritual, but simply springs from a character that has at last arrived at the place where it shares in the divine nature of which the author was speaking, the divine nature of the God who is love, according to another New Testament voice (1 John 4:8, 16). Our text assures us that, "as these things belong to and abound among you, they will ensure that you are not unproductive or unfruitful in regard to your acknowledgment of our Lord Jesus Christ" (2 Pet 1:8).

*   *   *

Is it so vitally important to be productive, to be fruitful? Can't I just believe and add salvation to all the other goodies I'm accumulating in this life? Can't I just hold on to my faith while investing the lion's share of my energy, time, and attention in things in the world that appeal to me at the moment? I don't find Scripture answering those questions in the affirmative. Some preachers and theologians will (though perhaps not when the questions are posed so bluntly), but it strikes me as *really* important that Scripture doesn't. Consider that very familiar parable that Jesus spoke concerning seeds and soils (Mark 4:1–20). Bearing fruit—being productive of the qualities and of the good consequences that are to characterize the new life—seems to be the decisive issue. If the pressures of one's peers or if the worries and interests of the world prevent that seed from reaching maturity and fruit bearing, Jesus writes off those seeds as a loss.

Our text answers these questions even more sharply: "For the people in whom these things are lacking are so short-sighted as to be blind, putting out of their minds the cleansing of their past sins" (2 Pet 1:9). It's not the kindest image to use—"so short-sighted as to be blind"—but it's an apt image nonetheless. One of the greatest threats to our ability to "bring all diligence to bear" in cultivating the life that Christ died to free us to live is the business of today, day after day (and, truth be told, the *non*business of today, day after day, for which we throw away each day just the same). We're called to be farsighted people, people that live with our eyes on the horizon of the dawning day of Christ's appearing. People who live with their eyes fixed *there* arrange their whole lives so as to be found blameless, even to be celebrated, on that day—to hear the words known from another familiar parable, "Well done, good and faithful servant!" (Matt 25:21, 23). To keep investing the lion's share of our attention and efforts today on pursuits and distractions that will not matter on *that* day—what better label could the author give this than the severest form of myopia?

The author adds a further indictment, however. To fail to move forward along this evacuation route and instead to splash around in the puddles along the roadside is to forget the costly investment that Jesus made in you to set you on this path in the first place. Forgetfulness of the benefits one had been given was considered a deplorable failure in the author's world. As Cicero, a Roman senator and statesman from the mid–first-century BC, wrote: "All people despise forgetfulness of benefactions, thinking it to be a personal injury against themselves since it discourages generosity; they regard the ingrate as an enemy to everyone who stands in need."[2] Similarly, Seneca, writing a century later: "The person who fails to make a return for a gift is ungrateful, but the person who has forgotten a gift once given is the most ungrateful of all. ... Who is more ungrateful than the person who has so fully put out of his mind the gift that ought to have remained foremost on his mind, that he has lost all knowledge of it?"[3]

* * *

According to our text, there's really only one response to God's gifting that makes any sense, one response that springs from keeping firmly in mind our past cleansing from sin, that great gift that calls for great gratitude in response, for living the life for which that cleansing was provided:

> Therefore, brothers and sisters, invest yourselves fully in making your calling and selection certain. For by doing these things you will certainly never trip up. For in this way entrance into the eternal kingdom of our Lord and Savior Jesus Christ will be richly supplied to you. (2 Pet 1:10–11)

Rather than asking the graceless question "How much or how little do I have to do to really be saved?" live the grace-full

---

2. *De officiis* 2.63 (my translation).
3. *De beneficiis* 3.1.3, 3.2.1 (my translation).

response. Make your calling and selection by God secure—not by some lazy theological argument by which you think to excuse yourself from pursuing God's evacuation route, but by that embodied response to God's calling and selection that makes of you a person who belongs in the eternal kingdom of our Lord Jesus Christ, in that place where "righteousness is at home" (2 Pet 3:13), by giving yourself over to pursuing the path along which all the provisions of "his divine power" naturally and rightly impel you. Here, for the author, is the surest foundation for any doctrine of assurance: "By doing these things you will *surely* not trip up" on the way to that kingdom.

25

"The Least Valued, the Most Honored"

Revelation 7:9–17; Mark 10:28–31

R evelation is a book to which Christians either give way too *much* or way too *little* attention. But even for churches that normally give it little attention, the ones that follow the Revised Common Lectionary—Episcopal, Lutheran, Presbyterian, many United Methodist congregations—will hear this passage read in their churches, generally on All Saints Day, occasionally at funerals or memorial services:

> I looked, and there was a great multitude that no one could count, from every nation, from all tribes and peoples and languages, standing before the throne and before the Lamb, robed in white, with palm branches in their hands. They cried out in a loud voice, saying, "Salvation belongs to our God who is seated on the throne, and to the Lamb!" ... Then one of the elders addressed me, saying, "Who are these, robed in white, and where have they come from? ... These are they who have come out of the great ordeal; they have washed their robes and made them white in the blood of the Lamb. For this

> reason they are before the throne of God, and worship him
> day and night within his temple, and the one who is seated
> on the throne will shelter them." (Rev 7:9–10, 13–15 NRSV)

John the Seer gives us a beautiful vision of the Church Triumphant, that innumerable company of those whom Jesus has ransomed from every nation, every people group, every language, every tribe, who now stand confident and victorious before God and God's Messiah, to whom they were faithful and obedient in life, and who now honor and care for these saints on the other side of death.

I know how those popular Bible prophecy "experts"—whose books flood our bookstores, whose interpretations flood our cable channels (I think you have to surf all the way up into the 300s or 400s, but they're there), whose failed predictions never seem to convince them or their audiences to give it a rest—I know how they talk about the people in this picture. They latch on to the clause "these are the ones who have come out of the Great Tribulation." Now, the NRSV translates this as "out of the great ordeal," but it could be rendered "the Great Tribulation," and this phrase is very important in the end-times schemes of these prophecy experts. The most common view, greatly popularized by the Left Behind series, is that genuine Christians will be raptured—caught up to heaven—at the start of the end times and will be rescued thereby from the troubles to come. Those nominal Christians who did not get raptured (and many prophecy experts would probably point to us as candidates), along with others who will become Christian during the end times, will have to face the Great Tribulation, the global persecution of Christians by the machine of the antichrist that will break forth in that last grim countdown to Armageddon.

*　　*　　*

Now, while I have many reservations about this popular approach to interpreting Revelation, my greatest reservation today is that it entirely ignores—and draws Christians' attention away from—the Great Tribulation happening *right now* to genuine, faithful Christians across the globe while it promises some rapture that, while it might get us out of costly faithfulness, will be far too late to spare them their strenuous contest to remain faithful under the stress and distress of the hostile forces of their societies and families. Many millions of Christians live under conditions of hostile persecution; tens of thousands are killed each year as a direct result of being identified or acting out their calling as Christians.

Often it is the immediate family of a convert to Christianity who express the greatest hostility and exert the most pressure. One member's defection to an alien religion (ours) brings shame upon the entire family, which regains its honor only by expelling—frequently, in some places, by murdering—the offending family member.

Often it is the authorities representing the dominant (or would-be dominant) religion from which the Christians have converted. We have heard a great deal about the brutality of radical Islamists as they murdered, execution-style and on video, Christians in Iraq and Syria who would not renounce their faith in favor of Islam and ISIS's vision of a pure Islamic State. Muslims who convert to Christianity face the harshest persecution and, not infrequently, martyrdom across the belt of Islamic lands. Christians in the villages of India increasingly face physical violence, sometimes resulting in death, at the hands of radical Hindus who crusade for a Hindu India. Most surprisingly, given the teachings of the Buddha, Buddhist monks have been at the heads of angry mobs that come to break up church meetings, threaten and beat pastors, and sometimes even burn churches in the rural areas of Sri Lanka. The monks fear their own loss of influence as individuals and families convert, while they and many of their villagers are driven by the conviction that Buddhism is the only proper faith for their island nation.

Sometimes the persecution of Christians is systematically pursued by the state itself. North Korea, where the worship of the ruling family as divine is mandatory, is an extreme example. Christians must hide their faith completely or risk being informed against, even by members of their own household. Many die of exhaustion in labor camps or of torture in prison. Some are able to escape through South Korea, sharing their stories and those of the dead and imprisoned.

The message of persecution is simple and straightforward: "We strongly disapprove of what you've become. You used to be an honorable member of our family, our village, our nation. We used to look at you as someone that we could count on to do the right thing, to affirm the same values that we hold dear, to be a valuable person. That's all changed now." Persecution aims first to reclaim the deviants, to bring converts to Christianity back to an acceptable way of living, the way the vast majority of the people in that area live. If that aim fails, persecution aims to eliminate an undesirable element and strongly discourage anyone thinking about becoming Christian from following through.

*   *   *

Some among John's churches were trying to live out their faith in the midst of significant pressures to cease and desist; others among John's churches were trying to adapt their faith so as to accommodate their neighbors' expectations of them as good citizens. From beginning to end in Revelation, John seeks to drive home a critically important message to both kinds of Christians, encouraging all of them together to live out an uncompromised witness to the One God and his Messiah. That message is also simple: Your neighbors, your family, your associates—those to whom you used to look for affirmation and support—may think of you now as among the least valuable, even value*less*, people around them. God, however, holds you in the highest esteem. You are the ones who have kept faith with Jesus, who have put obedience to God's commandments above everything else, including your personal comfort, safety, even life itself. In God's eternity, that esteem will be forever manifest to all.

If you were to read through the New Testament from start to finish with our globally persecuted sisters and brothers firmly fixed in your mind, you would probably be astonished to discover just how much of the New Testament speaks today specifically to *them*, how much its authors were concerned with the kinds of situations and challenges that they face (in large measure because their situation is often similar to—and in a great many cases substantially worse than—the situation of the early church under the Roman Empire, which our New Testament authors were directly addressing in the first century). It speaks to them of their honor in God's sight. It speaks of their suffering as an opportunity with which God has *graced* them, such that they have the chance to show Jesus the same commitment and investment that Jesus showed toward us all. It speaks of the eternal rewards such commitment will win for them, with Jesus testifying as a character witness on their behalf at the last judgment itself.

In quite a few places, the New Testament speaks to Christians who are free from such unwanted negative attention about those who suffer such persecution. For example, the author of the Letter to the Hebrews urges his hearers:

> Keep loving one another with the fervency of brothers
> and sisters. Don't neglect opportunities to show hospital-
> ity, for some have entertained angels in this way without
> knowing it. Be as mindful of those in prison as you would
> be if you were in the cell with them; be as mindful of
> those who are being physically abused as you would be
> if you were in their very bodies. (Heb 13:1–3)

That's admittedly an expanded translation, but I think it captures the sense of the original. Why would this author want to
focus Christians who are free from experiencing persecution
so strongly on reaching out to those Christians whom society
has most marginalized, most targeted? The obvious answer is
probably the correct one—the latter are those in the direst need
of help, encouragement, and reminders that they are loved and
that they are not alone or forgotten. They need more than ever
to know that their Christian family is a *real* family that will stand
by them. This in turn will also encourage them that the head of
this Christian family is *real*, will stand by them, and will deliver
on the rest of his promises to them.

I say "the rest of his promises" because the promise of a new
family, whose love and encouragement would be unfailing, is one
of Jesus' promises to his followers, one that will either prove true
or prove false within the span of this earthly life. This brings
us at last to today's Gospel reading. After the familiar episode of
the rich young man who could not leave his possessions behind
to follow Jesus,

> Peter began to say to [Jesus], "Look, we have left every-
> thing and followed you." Jesus said, "Truly I tell you,
> there is no one who has left house or brothers or sisters
> or mother or father or children or fields, for my sake
> and for the sake of the good news, who will not receive a

hundredfold now in this age—houses, brothers and sisters, mothers and children, and fields, *with persecutions*—and in the age to come eternal life." (Mark 10:28–31 NRSV, emphasis mine)

Many early Christians knew the pain of being rejected by their families for their new faith and practice, but they found a new family with each other. They embraced and held on to one another as fully and as firmly as brothers and sisters related by blood would be expected to do. When some were in special need, others would share their resources with them, just like brothers and sisters related by blood would be expected to do. When they forgot to love one another, hold on to one another, and support one another in this way, they would get another letter or other writing of what would become our New Testament telling them that they needed to love and support and come to one another's aid just like brothers and sisters related by blood would be expected to do. Jesus' promise to his followers *had* to prove true, and it would only prove true if Jesus' followers obeyed his command: "Love one another as I have loved you."

* * *

Is Jesus' promise still proving true in our setting? More to the point, is it going to prove true for Christians facing significant persecution in *other* settings? Will our sisters and brothers who have had to "let goods and kindred go," will the families of the martyrs who gave up "this mortal life also,"[1] find Jesus' promise in this paragraph to prove true?

Think for a moment how you would race about to rally both national and international attention and pressure were your

1. These lines come from the first stanza of Martin Luther's "A Mighty Fortress Is Our God," trans. Frederick H. Hedge (1853).

natural brother or sister, child or parent hauled off to a North
Korean labor camp or imprisoned for "blasphemy" in Pakistan;
how you would find your speediest way to comfort a natural
brother or sister, child or parent dispossessed of home and goods
and discovered living in a makeshift refugee camp just across a
border in a safe zone; how you would put yourself out to rescue
a family member from imminent danger or, if that proved impossible, to stand by him or her in that danger and bring whatever
relief in the midst of it that you could. Now think about the
degree to which you've exerted yourself for brothers and sisters, children and parents whom the Lord Jesus has united to
you as your family, those who will be your family forever. Have
you placed more or less value, by comparison, on the bond that
Christ's blood creates than you would on the bond that *ordinary*
blood creates? To what degree have you prioritized proving
Jesus' promise to Christians who have left family, home, *all* to
follow him to be trustworthy?

The author of Hebrews wrote to his congregations: "Keep
loving one another with the fervency of brothers and sisters."
Make this new family joined together by Christ prove more dura-
ble, more valuable, more reliable than the human families that
have rejected individual converts to Christianity. Make it more
real not only for them but for you as well, as you step out in
faith toward them, as you invest yourself in them, as you connect with them.

In our congregation, we observe the "International Day of
Prayer for the Persecuted Church" as an opportunity to remind
ourselves of and pray concerning the plight of our persecuted
sisters and brothers around the world. But now I'm asking each
one of you to give the situation of your brothers and sisters
across the world such regular attention that an annual reminder
will become superfluous. I'm asking you to take certain action

steps as a result of being a part of this morning's worship ser-vice—a public gathering with fellow Christians loudly prais-ing the name of Christ that will have no negative repercussions for you, your goods, or your family. Spend some time this week connecting with the members of our family in Christ whose profession of Jesus and whose attempts to obey him cost them dearly.

Here are a few recommendations to get you started. Take an hour or two off from Facebook this week, and spend some time exploring the websites of three organizations whose mission is to educate Christians in the West about the plight of their sisters and brothers in restricted nations and to connect persecuted Christians with the spiritual, material, and legal assistance that they need to persevere in their faith and witness and to know that the global family of God stands by them in their trials. Go to the Open Doors site and read their overview of the situation of Christians in each of the fifty countries most oppressive or least hospitable toward Christians. Go to the Voice of the Mar-tyrs and Barnabas Fund sites and read their news feeds of recent developments in the situation of particular Christian commu-nities or even particular Christian families in repressive coun-tries. Read the testimonies of Christian workers and disciples who have survived—or whose faith, at least, survived—violent persecution.[2] Learn about the many avenues these organizations give you to come to the aid of our blood brothers and sisters in Christ.

Pray. Each of these websites provides excellent suggestions for *how* to pray; as you yourself learn more about the plight of

2. Open Doors: https://www.opendoorsusa.org; Voice of the Martyrs: https://www.persecution.com; Barnabas Fund (a.k.a. Barnabas Aid): https://barnabasfund.org.

Christians in one or another country, that will also help guide you as you pray. Educate yourselves and one another, and keep learning. Get involved with at least one of these organizations, or find your own way to reach out and show the quality of love and degree of assistance that suits a brother or sister to some sector of the persecuted church. God has put it into our hands to bring significant relief to our family members in significant trouble and need. Raise awareness; rally support for those suffering the most extreme persecution by every venue available. Keep doing this homework that I'm assigning until you find yourself measuring up to the Scripture's benchmark for us: "Be as mindful of those in prison as you would be if you were in the same cell with them; be as mindful of those who are being physically abused as you would be if you were in their very bodies." Amen.

26

"The Lord's Prayer, the Disciples' Pledge"

Matthew 6:5–15

However varied Christian worship has become across denominations and across the millennia, almost all Christians know the Lord's Prayer and pray it regularly either in their congregations or in their personal prayer lives. During an internship as a hospital chaplain, standing beside the beds (in some cases, the death beds) of patients from the whole spectrum of Christian churches, I could always unite in prayer with these patients and their families using the Lord's Prayer. Indeed, when we pray this text, we unite our voices with saints from every Christian tradition in every age.

The fact that we are sufficiently familiar with the Lord's Prayer to pray it from memory is a great asset, since we always have it on hand. But our familiarity can also prevent us from really listening to the prayer and allowing it to sink deep into our consciousness so as to shape our intentions and desires. I'd like to make some space for you this morning in which to listen afresh to what Jesus teaches us both to seek from God and to show forth in our living by means of this prayer he has given us.

* * *

Jesus tells us to address the God of the cosmos as "our Father." We are not slaves who must grovel before a master; we are not petitioners approaching an indifferent king. Jesus wants us to see God as Father and ourselves as God's children. He brings us near to God as members of God's family and encourages us to enjoy this intimate access to God. This God, however, is *our* Father, not *my* Father: from the start, Jesus reminds us of the larger, now global family of which we are a part—and that God cares as deeply for every member of a vast family as God does for me.

When we call God "Father," we acknowledge that God is parenting us anew. I am aware that, for some even within our own congregation, the father in their natural household has made the very image problematic. But to call God "Father" is not to attribute to God the hurtful and, in some cases, abusive behaviors of some natural fathers, in whom the image of God was as distorted by their own brokenness as it is in ourselves. For Jesus, this is a Father whose kindness and generosity toward God's children surpasses that of any earthly father:

> Is there anyone among you who, if your child asks for bread, will give a stone? Or if the child asks for a fish, will give a snake? If you then, who are evil, know how to give good gifts to your children, how much more will your Father in heaven give good things to those who ask him! (Matt 7:9–11)

This is a Father who gives a loving, generous, joy-filled welcome to the wayward child rather than a reluctant second chance after a stiff lecture (Luke 15:21–24). This is not a Father who sets us up for failure with impossible expectations but a Father who positions us to succeed in our coming to maturity as disciples and who will provide whatever it takes to help us get there. As Jesus reminds us, "Don't be afraid, little flock, because it *pleases* the Father to give you the kingdom" (Luke 12:32).

To call God "Father" is also a pledge to grow more like him, to reflect his loving, generous, and righteous character more and more as we allow God's Holy Spirit to lead us into the likeness of the Father's perfect Son. The maxim "like father, like son" captures the direction in which the apostle Paul would impel us who call God "Father": "Be imitators of God, therefore, as dearly loved children and live a life of love" (Eph 5:1).

*   *   *

I once heard a pastor suggest, attempting to modernize the first petition ("Hallowed be thy name"), that we should pray "Holy be your Name." God's name, however, is *already holy*. What we pray here is for more people, in ever-widening circles, to recognize and revere the holiness of God's name. While this prayer will ultimately be fulfilled when God judges the world and reveals God's glory (Rev 14:7; 15:4), it finds fulfillment now chiefly through the behavior of those who are identified as God's people.

Where God's people fail to honor God with their own commitment to do what pleases God, those who look on, who know God only through his effect on us and our lives, lose respect for God. Paul wrote concerning his fellow Jews in this regard: "You who boast in the law, do you dishonor God by breaking the law? For, as it is written, 'The name of God is slandered among the gentiles because of you'" (Rom 2:23–24; quoting Isa 52:5). By contrast, when people who associate themselves with God's name do what is good, generous, noble, or otherwise reflective of God's virtuous character, those who witness their behavior think more highly of the God in whose name they do these things:

"Let your light shine before others, so that they may see your good works and give glory to your Father in heaven" (Matt 5:16; see also 1 Pet 2:12). When we pray, then, that God's name be revered as the holy name that it is, we pledge ourselves so to speak and act that we will give people no occasion to speak ill of our Lord and every occasion to acknowledge that there is something to this Jesus.

* * *

The second petition—"Thy kingdom come"—takes us to the heart of Jesus' own proclamation of God's kingdom, God's new ordering of human affairs to establish justice and wholeness throughout human community. This was good news for all who found themselves hemmed in and pressed down by the domination systems of the day but bad news for those who willingly participated in and profited from those systems. God's kingdom would not come in gently alongside oppressive arrangements. It necessarily upsets the way this world is ordered; it will put an end to every power that plunders and slaughters and calls it "government" or makes a desert and calls it "peace."[1]

This petition is the Christian's first pledge of allegiance. We ask God to expose our cooperation with any and all oppression and commit to relinquishing any privileges that are purchased at the cost of another's harm. We pledge ourselves to reorder our lives more and more in line with God's kingdom values and to call others to do the same, allowing God's politics and God's economy to shape our lives more and more and our temporary nation's politics and economy to shape our lives less and less so that, when Christ *does* come to inaugurate his kingdom, we will already be found among its citizens.

1. Tacitus, *Agricola* 30.

* * *

The Gospels give us a dramatic picture of what it means to wrestle with the next petition ("Thy will be done, on earth as it is in heaven") when Jesus returns to this particular prayer in the garden of Gethsemane. Praying that God's will be done means putting God's purposes ahead of our own preferences, God's desires ahead of our own agendas. But to call Jesus "Lord" without being willing to do this is meaningless (Matt 7:21). Everything in heaven—the orderly activity of angelic hosts, the stars moving in their courses, the progression of seasons—moves in tune with the decrees set for them by the Almighty. It is only "earth," the human sphere, that is out of step with God, where God must reassert his leadership.

We pledge ourselves, with this petition, to find our proper place as God's creatures in God's cosmos, in the seeking and doing of the will of the One who made us for his good pleasure. How different from the prayers of "help me get my way," "make everything turn out the way I want it to," and "bless my projects" that we are so often disposed to offer! But the more we are able to internalize this petition—"Thy will be done"—the more complete our journey to maturity in Christ.

* * *

"Give us this day our ration of bread." When it comes to setting our expectations and even our desires for a share in this world's goods, Jesus directs us toward extreme modesty. Jesus reminds us of God's provision of manna in the wilderness, enough for everyone, every day—and anything hoarded for the next day turned to maggots! While this petition keeps me mindful of the fact that all the nourishment my family and I enjoy each day is a gift from God and is to be received with gratitude, we are so far from being in danger of not getting meat, fruit, vegetables, and snacks for the next year—let alone "daily bread"—that the petition seems quaint. At the same time, for so many, what a gift it would be to have bread *today*! What an unthinkable blessing it would be to be assured of its being supplied tomorrow!

As I pray this petition, I remember that I do not pray it alone, nor only on my behalf. My sisters and brothers in Christ in South Sudan, in refugee camps throughout the world, in nations where confessing the faith means economic embargo, pray it as well. Their petitions convict me of my plenty. If they are part of the "us" for whom we pray "Give us this day our daily bread," has God already answered their prayer in what we hold in our possession? The failure may not be in God's giving, but in our distribution of those gifts. Does God regard the treasures we have stashed away for ourselves as the equivalent of containers of food and supplies rotting in a warehouse while nearby populations die for want of food and medicine? This petition is also, really, our pledge to be sure that all of God's family are receiving their daily bread.

*   *   *

The next petition makes the pledge related to our plea explicit: when we ask God to "forgive us our trespasses as we forgive"—or, in Matthew, "as we *have forgiven*"—"those who trespass against us," Jesus forces us to acknowledge that our forgiveness of others is really prerequisite to praying for our own forgiveness. If we collect the texts in the Gospels about forgiveness, we find something of a circle of forgiveness being set in motion. God forgives us our offenses against God's dignity. We, in response, forgive those who injure our sense of our honor, worth, and deserving in one form or another. Because we are faithful to our obligation to imitate God's character, we dare to come again to God asking forgiveness for our further offenses against him. In the parable of the unforgiving servant (Matt 18:21–35), Jesus teaches that the requirement to forgive as we have been forgiven is simply a matter of mathematics. Our sins have cost God so much more than other people's sins against us have cost us that we would offer God the greatest insult of all by holding onto our grudges against other human beings after expecting God to get over our affronts to him.

Forgiving is difficult. Sometimes it's difficult simply because we're so prideful. Where this is the case, we need to reread the parable of the unforgiving servant until we understand that, if God can forgive us our affronts against his honor, we can forgive other people. But sometimes it's difficult because we have been so deeply hurt, betrayed, or demeaned. This, too, is not foreign to God, whom *we* betray whenever we choose pleasing ourselves over pleasing the One who gives us the gift of each day's life. What God commands, God will also empower. If we cannot pray this petition as people who have already "forgiven those who have trespassed against us," we can pray for God's help to come to the place where, having been so loved and healed by God's Spirit, we can forgive and move forward in freedom. The importance of our forgiving, however, is underscored most dramatically by this simple fact: this is the only petition in the prayer on which Jesus himself commented at the end (Matt 6:14–15)!

* * *

The final, complementary pair of petitions—"Don't lead us into situations that will tempt or test us, but deliver us from the Evil One"—may seem odd at first. Do we really expect *God* to lead us into temptation? That's the role of Satan, "the Evil One." It's the role of the world around us shaped by him, and the role of our own wayward yearnings. The sense may be made clearer when we think of Jesus rousing the sleepy disciples in Gethsemane and telling them to pray "that they come not into the time of trial" (Matt 26:41). That time certainly was coming; the question was whether they would remain faithful through it on the other side.

In this petition, we pray to the God who knows us better than we know ourselves, who discerns our weaknesses from afar, and who may exercise our faith so as to make it stronger but who will not allow us to be tempted beyond our capacity. When we pray this petition, we ask of God: "Don't ever bring us where our faith will falter." This does not always mean places of adversity. Prosperity can be just as destructive to faith, if not more so, putting those things that are distracting and destructive to our souls more easily within our grasp. It is also the pledge of our hearts to seek the way of faithfulness in the midst of temptation and to turn aside from temptation, as soon as we recognize it as such, as the way in which God is *not* leading us. We commit to God our complete allegiance: if we seek rescue from the Evil One, we will not, at the same time, flirt with his enticements.

* * *

The words of praise with which we conclude our prayer were not originally spoken by Jesus, but they were being added at the end of the Lord's Prayer even before the church got out of the first century.[2] And it is indeed a fitting conclusion, as we affirm the surpassing power of God to bring about all for which we have just prayed and to empower us to keep all to which we have pledged ourselves: to bring ever-greater honor to God's name as we honor God with our witness and service; to give ourselves ever more fully to the doing of *God's* will and to making

2. See, for example, the version of the Lord's Prayer in the *Didache*, a late first- or early second-century handbook on Christian faith, liturgical practice, and ethics (especially *Didache* 8.2).

his kingdom visible and real among us; to seek God's supply of daily bread for God's *entire* household; to extend forgiveness in recognition of God's forgiveness of us; and to follow God's leading toward, and to seek God's empowerment for, faithfulness in the face of every temptation and trial. Amen.

27

"Knowing Christ"[1]

Philippians 3:2–11; John 17:1–8, 25–26

Paul's letter to the Christians in Philippi is one of his most personal. It's written to a congregation that, unlike the congregations in Galatia and Corinth, really seems not to have given Paul much trouble. The Philippian Christians weren't tossed this way and that in their loyalty—now toward Paul, now toward more recent teachers telling them something different and calling Paul's message and authority into question. This congregation was remarkably supportive of Paul, both in his missionary work and in his imprisonment—and Paul trusted this congregation enough to accept their support, something he did *not* do in regard to the Christians in Corinth, since they seem to have been in danger of thinking that would have put the apostle in their pocket. Indeed, Paul's Letter to the Philippians exists because the congregation sent a little something to Paul

---

1. This and the following two sermons are based on the mission statement of Port Charlotte United Methodist Church: *Know* Christ; *Grow* more like Christ; *Go* to serve Christ.

through one of their members, Epaphroditus, who apparently also filled Paul in on what was going on in the congregation.

And so, in the course of addressing his friends in Philippi, Paul writes his most intensely personal testimony concerning his own experience of coming to Christ, the realignment of his values that that experience provoked, and his driving passion ever since:

> Beware the dogs! Beware the wicked workers! Beware the flesh-cutters! For *we* are the circumcision, we who are worshiping in God's Spirit and grounding our worth in Christ Jesus, and not putting our confidence in flesh— even though I have grounds for confidence in flesh. If anyone else thinks to have grounds for confidence in flesh, I have more—circumcised on the eighth day; belonging to the tribe of Benjamin; a Hebrew born from Hebrews; in regard to the law, a Pharisee; in regard to zealous commitment, a persecutor of the church; in regard to alignment with the law, blameless! But what-ever things were once a credit to me, these things I have written off as a loss on account of Christ. Indeed, I put everything in the debit column when set against the surpassing value of knowing Christ Jesus, my Lord—on whose account I have been debited in regard to every-thing, and I count all of it as trash, so that I might gain Christ, and so that I might be found in him, not having the righteousness that I could establish for myself in line with the law, but having the righteousness that comes from trusting Christ, the righteousness that God provides on the basis of trust—to know him and the power of his rising from the dead and partnership with him in his

sufferings, being made like him as he showed himself to
be in his dying, if somehow I might arrive at the resurrection from the dead. (Phil 3:2–11)

For reasons that are not entirely clear, Paul launches off into a
rant against a group of rival teachers that have been active in
his mission field. He took on teachers of this sort in Galatia; it
is not clear whether he thinks, years later now, that they might
show up in Philippi, or whether he is just using them as a good
example of how *not* to do Christianity. Whatever the reason for
bringing them up, their example is clearly one *not* to imitate.
They haven't discovered the surpassing value of knowing Christ;
they still think that the fact of their circumcision, their being
a part of the historic people of God, and their being born and
carved into the covenant of Israel is the high-water mark of
religion, with Christ being a winsome add-on but not a game-
changing, life-changing, value-changing tidal wave.

Paul knows exactly where these rival teachers are coming
from. In fact, nobody knows better the fulfillment that could
come through being a Torah-observant member of the covenant with Israel than Paul—"circumcised on the eighth
day; belonging to the tribe of Benjamin; a Hebrew born from
Hebrews; in regard to the law, a Pharisee; in regard to zealous
commitment, a persecutor of the church; in regard to alignment with the law, blameless!" So much for the idea that the
problem with the Jewish law is that it was impossible to keep
it; Paul seems to think he had done just fine on that score.
The problem with the way of life that had been regulated by
the Torah is that Paul discovered—only by virtue of having
been filled by his experience of Jesus' love and the Holy Spirit's
friendship—how empty, how poor, by comparison, his life had
been. As he would put it, somewhat differently, in his second

surviving letter to the Corinthians, "What had been glorious was shown to have no glory in comparison with the surpassing glory" of Christ (2 Cor 3:10).

Paul was willing to set all of that aside, to be stripped of all the security and status he enjoyed in his circles of Pharisaic Judaism:

> "But whatever things were once a credit to me, these things I have written off as a loss on account of Christ. Indeed, I put everything in the debit column when set against the surpassing value of knowing Christ Jesus, my Lord—on whose account I *have* been debited in regard to everything, and I count all of it as trash, so that I might gain Christ." (Phil 3:7–8)

Paul's driving passion was now "to know him and the power of his rising from the dead and partnership with him in his sufferings" (Phil 3:10). It is important for us to realize that he is writing these words at least twenty years after his initial encounter with the living Christ. Two decades later, getting closer and deeper in his knowledge of Jesus and his experience of Jesus' fellowship is still that one thing to which *everything* else takes a back seat.

Is that *your* passion?

Do you know Jesus well enough to know that you can't get enough of Jesus? To want to know him more, and to want this enough that you make the room to know him more?

*　*　*

We have decided, by virtue of the opening clause of the mission statement that we adopted several years ago, to keep the value of knowing Christ in the front and center of our lives together in this congregation: "KNOW Christ." This first imperative drives us toward a deeper knowledge of who Christ is and what Christ wants. Indeed, though I understand that we needed to limit the mission statement to catchy sound bites, we really are impelled to seek out a deeper knowledge of God in all *three* persons—Father, Son, and Holy Spirit. This knowing is shaped by *information*, by learning more about our heavenly Father, the divine Son incarnate in Jesus, and the empowering and guiding Spirit, such as study of the Scriptures provides. But this knowing must also shape, be shaped by, *relationship*, by making room for regular, personal encounter with the God who encounters us. It was about the value of this informed, relational knowing of the Son that Paul wrote so passionately. Experiencing—knowing—God is the bedrock of Christian life; experiencing—knowing—God *together* is the bedrock of Christian community.

What are you willing to "write off as a loss for the sake of the surpassing value of knowing Christ Jesus," our Lord? Do you have the "surpassing value" in view as you come here to worship on Sunday morning? Paul was willing to sacrifice religion for relationship, specifically relationship with Christ Jesus our Lord.

Don't misunderstand me. I'm all about liturgy and the spiritually formative power of the traditions of Christian worship as we allow liturgy to shape us, as we embrace the various components of liturgy as the spiritual equivalent of a balanced diet or a complete weight-training circuit. But the point of coming here this morning is not in the performance of the prayers, the hymns, the anthem, the sermon. The point is not in the *form* of what we do but in *whom* we come to encounter, so that we can leave knowing about him, and knowing him, a little more. It is not in the "what's next?" in the bulletin, but in the "how will I open up my soul even more to God in what's next?" Don't settle for the religion, but strive, at every point, after the relationship.

Paul didn't just share his heart for knowing Christ Jesus because he was feeling warm and close to the Philippian Christians. He wanted to change something in their congregation. A chapter before our focal paragraph, Paul urges his friends: "In humility, think of one another as possessing greater dignity than yourselves; don't look after what is in your own interest, but after what is in the other's interest" (2:3-4). If you read on just a bit past our focal paragraph, you come across this topic again, and more pointedly: "I urge Euodia and I urge Syntyche"—two leading women whom Paul considers coworkers—"to agree in the Lord, and I urge you, my genuine yokefellow, to help them" come to terms with each other rather than continuing to cherish their grudge and to foster division in the body (4:2-3).

Paul's sharing of his own testimony—his willingness to "write everything off as a loss for the sake of the surpassing value of knowing Christ Jesus"—has some clear implications for the disagreements his friends are having amongst themselves. "If you know the value of what you come together to seek out, you'll recognize that whatever is getting in the way of knowing Christ together is just so much rubbish—and you'll toss out your personal 'trash' for the sake of attaining, together, what is so much more valuable for all of you."

Let me move from preaching into meddling. The guys who keep their hats on in church. The blip in the sound system or mix-up in the screens. The blasted music director choosing yet *another* unfamiliar hymn. The inappropriateness of someone's dress. The sixty-*first* minute of the worship service. The value of what you're holding on to, if it's anything like *any* of these things, pales in comparison with the value of what you could be reaching for, together, in this place. Are you willing to set it aside as something of no account for the sake of the surpassing value of knowing Christ Jesus and for the sake of not allowing yourself to distract yourself from laying hold of that greater good?

*   *   *

Paul, of course, was not just a seeker of Christ on Sundays. His passion for knowing Christ Jesus spilled all over his calendar. Granted, Paul was a bit of a fanatic when it came to knowing Jesus and making Jesus known, but nevertheless let's allow his example to challenge us. What are you doing whenever you're not making the time to know more about Jesus and to experience Jesus' friendship and conversation? It'll never be worth more, but is it at least necessary? Important? We will, none of us, probably ever be willing to count *everything* as so much rubbish for the sake of the surpassing value of knowing Christ Jesus our Lord, but are we willing at least to count *some* things as rubbish and clear out *some* of the trash in our week for the sake of seeking a fuller knowledge of him and seeking to know him more fully? What will your Monday, what will your Tuesday, say to God about how much you understand the value—the surpassing value—of knowing him, of the invitation God has given to *you* to know him, to be known by him, to know yourself as you are known by him?

Our most basic currency as mortals is not money but time. I've found out over the years that I can pretty much always make more money, but I can't make any more time. It's our most precious commodity, and yet we will all spend the same amount of it every single day. There's no saving it up, and there's frankly no way to know when it will be used up. In the midst of his prayer on behalf of his disciples on the eve before his passion, Jesus said, "This is eternal life"—this is *unending* life, this is life *without limits*—"that they might know you, the only genuine God, and Jesus Christ, whom you sent" (John 17:3). We step out of the constant dripping away of time and into that life that knows no ending at any point that we find ourselves in touch with the only genuine God and with Jesus Christ.

We're careful bargain hunters when it comes to our money, but we can be terrible shoppers when it comes to our time—buying an hour on Netflix rather than an hour of eternity in the presence of God; buying an hour on social media feeds rather than an hour being fed by the Bread of Life; buying an hour of browsing in a mall rather than an hour of allowing the Holy Spirit to browse *us*, strengthening the work of Christ in us and relaxing the hold of the flesh over us; trading an hour for a manicure but reluctant to spend an hour on soul cure. Since we're going to spend the same amount of our limited time *every* day, let's be sure that we're getting the best value for it.

* * *

Perhaps many of you already do what I am about to recommend—in which case, may God keep you fervently in love with him so as to continue to do so. To the rest, I would urge each of you (each of *us*, to be perfectly honest) to set apart—to sanctify—times during each day for growing in your knowledge of God, both your knowledge about God and your experience of knowing God, of being present with God. A staple for such times would be the reading of Scripture, combined with prayerful conversation with God, with the living Christ, inviting the Holy Spirit to illumine both the text and you, in light of the text. It might also involve reading what those who have known God deeply and closely have written about knowing God deeply and closely— what we might call the devotional classics of the Christian faith.

It would surely involve prayer, preferably using different resources so as to open yourself up to God in different and, therefore, more complete ways. In my own life, the *Book of Common Prayer* has been indispensable in this regard, but you could also turn to collections of prayers such as *The Oxford Book of Prayer* and to the texts of many hymns that are essentially prayers set to music. The benefit of such resources is simple: we do not know everything that we ought to pray for or pray about; we are not always disposed to pray for all those things that we *do* know we ought to be praying for. These resources expand our conversation with God; they expand the dimensions of our knowing God and experiencing God. And the most critical of all components is waiting in patient silence for God, for Christ, to show up.

But experiencing God need not—indeed, should not—be limited to those hours (though we need those hours if we are to remain in the awareness of God's presence and companionship in other hours). The Triune God can be known in the midst of one's everyday activities as well. A great devotional classic in this regard is *The Practice of the Presence of God*, the compilation of notes taken by a certain abbot during several visits with a kitchen monk named Brother Lawrence, together with a series of letters written by Brother Lawrence to an inquiring layperson.

Paul came "to know Christ and the power of his rising from the dead and the fellowship of his sufferings" not only in private prayer but in the thick of his missionary work, his travels, his imprisonments and beatings, his teaching in the house churches, his leatherworking in the commercial market. We can as well if we keep our hearts and minds attuned to Christ and conversing with Christ in the midst of all those activities and occupations into which we would invite Christ.

Our mission statement is our constant memo to ourselves: "Know Christ." Keep writing off as a loss, and throwing aside as trash, everything that gets in the way of that pursuit. Keep spending your time in ways that reflect the all-surpassing value of knowing Christ. Amen.

28

"Growing More Like Christ"

Romans 8:28–29; Luke 6:27–36

It's a familiar saying from Scripture, perhaps one of the more frequently quoted from Paul's letter to the Christians in Rome: "All things work together for good." You've probably heard it from other Christians on several occasions. You shared the news that a job offer didn't come through. "Don't worry— all things work together for good. Something better will come along." You just broke up with a significant other. "I know it's hard, but you've got to remember—all things work together for good." You were just diagnosed with cancer. "Don't give up; God will get you through. All things work together for good."

Now in all these situations, the person pulling out that clause from Romans 8:28 means well, seeking to shine a ray of hope, an assurance of a brighter future, where a dark cloud has just settled over a friend or family member. Indeed, we can have confidence that God has our future—a good and bright one indeed— firmly in hand no matter what unwelcome circumstances settle upon us at any given time. But it's also good for us to listen to what Paul actually had in mind when he wrote those words, "All things work together for good," lest we think that the "good" that God cares about most is to bring us back to pleasant circumstances in *this* life rather than to fit us for glorious circumstances in the *next*. This is one of those many instances where a little attention to context brings a great deal of clarity.

> Now we know that, for those who persist in loving God, for those who are called in line with God's purpose, all things work together unto the good, because those whom God foreknew God also destined to be shaped into the likeness of his Son, in order that he might be the firstborn among many brothers and sisters. (Rom 8:28-29)

Paul has a very clear idea of "the good" that is the aim toward which all things, by God's providential ordering, are working—that we should be "shaped into the likeness of his Son," Jesus Christ, that there should be an unmistakable family resemblance between all of us and our eldest brother in God's household. God's overarching aim—and this for our ultimate good—is not to make us happy; it's not to make us prosperous; it's not to make all the troubles and heartaches of our lives go away. It *is* to make us more like Jesus, so that when he looks at us on the last day, he recognizes his Son, his Righteous One, in each one of us.

The Christian life must be a journey of change—specifically, change in the direction of becoming more and more like Christ. Paul was clear on this point throughout his writings: "Don't continue to be *con*formed to this age, but keep on being *trans*formed" (Rom 12:2). Every one of us is molded, is shaped, as we journey through life. Every one of us is conformed to some pattern. The question before us is: To what will we be conformed? In what direction will we be shaped? Am I going to step out of the ruts that the structures and the logic and the values of "this age" have dug out for me, to keep me inclined to go with its flow, to be the kind of person it wants and even needs for me to be? Am I going to step out into new paths, the path of being transformed in the direction of Christlikeness—ultimately, the path of reflecting the heart of God and responding from the heart of God? The world around me will keep applying its subtle pressures to conform to it so that I maintain it. I can yield to those pressures, or I can cooperate with God's Spirit as he applies his subtle pressures to transform me so that God can also keep breaking into this world, this age, and change it *through* me, starting by reclaiming the space in the world that *is* me—the sphere of my interactions with the world's inhabitants.

*   *   *

The first two clauses of our mission statement are: "KNOW Christ. GROW more like Christ." Paul's intensely personal testimony in Philippians resonates strongly with both: "I want to *know Christ* and the power of his resurrection and the fellowship of his sufferings, being *transformed into the likeness of his death*, so that I might somehow arrive at the resurrection from the dead" (Phil 3:11). Notice that, for Paul, the knowing and the growing are inseparable. Paul's passion to *know* Christ drove him in the direction of *growing* more like Christ, specifically "being transformed into the likeness of his death," being changed into a person who would give himself over for God's purposes, who would live with a view to accomplishing God's purposes for the other person and, thus, serving the interests of the other person rather than his own interests—which was precisely what Christ did in his death. This *growing*, in turn, opened up new dimensions of *knowing* Christ for Paul—for there can be no knowing "the fellowship of Christ's sufferings" apart from living in line with that "mind of Christ" who loved us and gave himself over for us.

In his second surviving letter to the Christians in Corinth, Paul creates a clever contrast between an episode in Moses' life and the essence of the Christian life. During the period in which God was giving the law to Moses, Moses would go up on Mount Sinai and sit in the presence of God. As a result, when Moses returned to the camp of the Hebrews, his face was glowing with the reflected glory of having been in God's presence. After Moses delivered the next installment of the law, he would put a veil over his face until the glow had faded away. It's different with us, Paul declared. As we keep spending time in the Lord's presence, the glory doesn't fade away. Indeed, we're not just glowing with a reflected glory, but our very face—the self we see in the mirror—is *becoming* the reflection of the One into whose face we are gazing. As Paul puts it, "We all, with our faces unveiled, gazing intently at the Lord's glory, are being transformed"—the Greek word Paul uses gives us our English word "metamorphosis"—"into the same image, from glory to glory, and all of this from the Lord, the Spirit" (2 Cor 3:18).

At the conclusion of his letter to the Christians in Galatia, Paul declared that it didn't mean anything in God's sight if a person was circumcised or not—that is, it didn't matter if a person was Jewish or had joined himself to the Jewish people or not. What mattered in God's sight was "a new creation" (Gal 6:15). From the rest of Galatians, we get a pretty good idea of what this "new creation" is. Paul himself had become a "new creation" as a result of the righteousness that God gives to those who trust Christ to align them with what God approves: "Through the law, I died to the law so that I might come alive to God. I was crucified together with Christ! It's no longer *me* living, but *Christ* living in me. The life I'm *now* living in the flesh, I'm living by trusting the Son of God who loved me and gave himself over for me" (Gal 2:19-20). This is precisely what Paul so earnestly seeks to bring into reality in and among his converts in Galatia, in regard to whom Paul finds himself at his wits' end—"My little children, with whom I am again in labor pains until Christ takes shape in and among you!" (Gal 4:19). Paul was after his own and his converts' complete metamorphosis. This was, for him, an indispensable facet of discipleship—indeed, the aim of all discipleship.

Is that your aim?

Is that where you are heading, seeking to move closer to that end day by day?

*   *   *

The second mandate in our mission statement—"GROW more like Christ"—drives us forward along this trajectory, urging us on to the disciplined "stripping off of the old person" that we used to be apart from Christ and the "putting on of the new person who is being made new again, reflecting the image of the Creator" (Col 3:8–15)—reflecting the image of Christ, "who is the image of the invisible God" (Col 1:15). Make no mistake: the goal is not merely to become a better person. The goal toward which God works, the goal for which Paul strove, is to bring Christ to life within us. The goal is to become a different person who is "Christ in you," which also gives us "the hope of glory" (Col 1:27). This is what the Holy Spirit works to bring into being in each of our lives and in our relationships with one another, making us more like Jesus, shaping us to embody him and his attitudes and values more and more.

Growing more like Christ requires a death to make room for a new life. It means our death to our own agendas, our own easily provoked ill feelings, our own vision for how we want our lives to go and everyone else to behave. It means coming alive to, and living for, God's agenda, acting and responding to the person in front of us on the basis of God's initiating love, giving our energies and time and resources over to God's vision for how God wants others' lives to go.

Jesus called his first followers to pursue this trajectory of growing more like God. Since we confess Jesus to be "the image of the invisible God," we can keep our mission statement, for to "GROW more like Christ" is to "GROW more like God." It is to have the divine image restored in us and freshly imprinted on all our actions and interactions. And so we read in the Gospel:

> I say to you who are listening: keep showing love to your enemies, keep doing good for those who hate you, keep blessing those who persist in cursing you, keep praying concerning those who are mistreating you. To the one striking you on the cheek, present also the other, and don't hold back your tunic from the one taking your outer cloak. Keep giving to those who ask, and don't demand that the person who takes your goods return them. And what you would desire that people should do toward you, keep doing this for them.
>
> Now if you continue to love those who keep showing you love, what kind of generosity are you showing? Don't even sinners continue to show love to those who love them? And if you do good for those who have been doing you good, what kind of generosity are you showing? Even sinners do as much. And if you lend to those from whom you hope to receive, what kind of generosity are you showing? Even sinners lend to sinners, to receive as much back again. But keep showing love to your enemies and doing good and lending, hoping for nothing, and your reward will be bountiful, and you will be children of the Most High—because he himself is generous to the ungracious and wicked. Persevere in being compassionate just as your Father is compassionate. (Luke 6:27–36)

To "GROW more like Christ" is also to live in line with his instructions, for if ever anyone practiced what he preached, it was Jesus! Who showed his enemies (including us, while we were still his enemies!) more love than Jesus did? Who prayed more powerfully for those who were mistreating him than Jesus did when he said, "Father, forgive them, for they don't know what they are doing" (Luke 23:34)? Who more than Jesus showed love and did good to those who had *not* first loved or done good to him?

*   *   *

My "old self" lives a narrow life, constrained on the one hand by my self-centered, self-serving, and self-vaunting drives and, on the other hand, by the good or by the lack of good that I encounter in others. The good that our old selves can do is generally limited by the good another has done (or might do); some words or actions of the other person can rather predictably provoke anger, enmity, or malice, as if the other person holds our strings. The old self can never rise to the measure of God's righteousness. But God's character—which is also the character we see in Jesus—is quite different. It is, indeed, "vast, boundless, free." It is independent of the good or lack of good in the other; it is so full and so complete that it can be "generous toward the ungracious and wicked," encountering the ungracious and the wicked with the transforming power that once encountered us when we were ungracious and wicked.

To know Christ is also to remain continuously tapped into God's fullness, God's completeness, as branches are tapped into and continually nourished and filled by the vine. It is to be empowered for Christlikeness, for acting and responding to those around us from God's compassionate and generous character in ways that would have been impossible, incomprehensible, and ultimately undesirable to our old selves.

I think that this is what is really meant by "justification"—not just being *declared* "innocent" because we have some pull with the Judge's Son but *becoming* just and good because God's Son now drives us in our inclinations, words, and deeds. I think that this is part of what Paul had in mind when he talked about "salvation"—not just being saved from the consequences of our past *sins* but being saved from our past *selves*, the source of those sins, to become something else, something more beautiful, something pleasing to God—to GROW more like Christ. This is what we pray for when we sing the final verse of Charles Wesley's hymn: "Finish then thy new creation! Pure and spotless let us be! Let us see thy great salvation" as we are "perfectly restored in thee." The image of God, which we bore in creation but lost in our fall, is restored in us by Christ, "who is the image of the invisible God" (Col 1:15), living in and through us. Amen.

* * *

Gazing into the face of the Savior,
    peering into his excellent ways,
We seek to be changed into his likeness
    and walk as he did all of our days.
Christ came to serve and used life for others,
    seeking our good and not his own:
He laid aside his rights and ambitions,
    and through his service made God's love known.

If we would be disciples of Jesus,
    we too shall seek not to be served, but serve
And do for all as God would have us,
    not as we wish or think they deserve.

We too are called to stop our processions
    and care for those in need on the road,
Knowing that this is what our God honors:
    not worldly greatness, but love bestowed.

God leaves us not alone on this journey:
    God's Holy Spirit he freely imparts,
Giving us as gifts to each other,
    Christ's love to service urging our hearts.
Let us then seek to be Christ's reflection,
    and spur each other on to ensure,
Each one equipping and serving the other,
    all reach Christ's stature, fully mature.[1]

---

1. This original poem provided the text for the choral anthem written to complement the sermon.

29

"Going to Serve Christ"

Hebrews 12:28–13:16

I t's easy to lose sight of the value of a particular gift. It's easy for that initial flood of surprise and delight to fade away. How many backs of closets, how many attics, how many yard sales are full of gifts that once enthralled us, then began their procession from the top of the desk or dresser where we could always access them, to the top drawer where we could reach for them occasionally, to the box in the closet, to the box in the garage, to Goodwill? How much dust has already settled on some of the gifts you just received this past Christmas?

The author of the Letter to the Hebrews writes to a group of Christians, some of whom at least have begun to lose sight of the value of a particular gift, others of whom might stand in similar danger. I say "danger" because there are some gifts that are so valuable or in which the giver is so personally invested that you don't dare let them find their way into the back of a closet, a box in the garage, or—heaven forbid—a yard sale. Now, I'm not talking about that hideous wind chime that you *have* to leave up because so-and-so gave it to you, and so-and-so comes over to your house every now and then and listens for it when there's a breeze. I'm talking about the gift that cost the giver a *lot*, that he or she acquired only with considerable care, labor, or expense; perhaps that he or she found it difficult to part with but did nevertheless as a sign of his or her affection for you. For such a gift to end up in a box in the garage or in a yard sale would surely damage the relationship, for the gift is so valuable that how it is treated becomes a symbol for the relationship itself.

Some of the Christians addressed by the Letter to the Hebrews were about ready to put this gift in the back of the closet, or even in the trash, because this was a gift that was costing them too much, in terms of their neighbors' goodwill, to keep displaying. I'm talking, of course, about the gift of reconciliation with the God of Israel, whom they had come to believe was the *only* God—the gift of reconciliation procured for them by Jesus at the cost of his own life—an expensive gift indeed. A great deal of the Letter to the Hebrews, in fact, is given over to reminding the audience of the immense value of what they have been given in Jesus, so as to embolden them to continue to bear the cost of displaying this gift where it would be visible to their neighbors, not least of all by continuing to associate openly with the other people in their city who gather in Jesus' name. They have the forgiveness of their sins and a fresh start with God; they have the assurance that God's Son will continue to direct God's favor in their direction as they face any difficulty or necessity; they have a place now in God's own household, God's own family; they have the unprecedented boldness to enter into heaven itself, the very presence of the Holy God, having been cleansed from every defilement by Jesus their high priest and atoning sacrifice, whenever that day comes when the way into heaven is disclosed; they have the promise of citizenship in God's eternal kingdom, a homeland that will embrace them forever.

* * *

And it is this that brings us to our focal passage:

> So then, since we are in the process of receiving a king-
> dom that cannot be shaken, let us show gratitude, and
> through the manifestation of this gratitude let us wor-
> ship God in a manner well-pleasing to him, with reverent
> submission and awe—for our God is indeed a consuming
> fire. (Heb 12:28–29)

The NRSV translates that first verse, "let us give thanks," the NIV,
"let us be thankful"; the CEB comes much closer to the meaning
of the Greek at this point with "let's continue to express our
gratitude." Let us treat these gifts and act toward the Giver in the
manner that will show him that we understand their value—and
that we value the relationship into which he has invited us by the
very act of giving us such precious gifts in the present and promises of gifts yet to come.

The ancient Greeks and Romans thought a great deal about
gift giving and gratitude and the quality of the relationships
that these exchanges created and maintained. Gratitude would
take certain, rather predictable forms, all of them considerably
more substantial than the perfunctory thank-you notes we had
to write out as kids to various uncles, aunts, and the like. If I
received a gift of significant value from someone, particularly
a gift the value of which I would likely never be able to match
in the future, I would show gratitude, in part, by bearing widespread witness to the gift and to the giver's virtue in giving it. In
his manual on giving and receiving gifts well, Seneca, a Roman
contemporary of Paul, wrote: "I shall never be able to repay you
my gratitude, but, at any rate, I shall at least not cease from

declaring *everywhere* that I am unable to repay it."[1] He advises giving testimony to "the blessing that has come to us by pouring forth our feelings and bearing witness—not merely in the hearing of the giver, but everywhere."[2] A gift that one would prefer to keep hidden from public view, hiding one's connection with the giver, one should never accept in the first place.[3] One would also be watchful for occasions on which to render some appropriate return for the gift—in investing oneself in advancing the giver's interests in the world, hence in service to the giver, if one was not in a position to give a gift of like value.

And so, quite directly, gratitude supplies the fundamental motivation that drives and shapes our response of witnessing to the Giver and looking for opportunities to serve the Giver's interests. The author of Hebrews helps his hearers make this very connection. In 12:28, he speaks of worshiping God in a way that will be "well pleasing" to God—that is, by allowing gratitude for God's gifts and promises to shape how they will live. Toward the end of this passage, in Hebrews 13:15–16, the author returns to naming those kinds of worship that are in fact "well pleasing" to God—the kinds of religious acts, the kinds of liturgical sacrifices, that show God the reverence and grateful service God's favors merit:

> Through Jesus Christ, therefore, let us continually offer to God the 'sacrifice of praise'—the fruit of lips that profess his name. Let us not overlook doing good and sharing, for sacrifices of this kind are well-pleasing to God. (Heb 13:16)

1. *On Benefits* 2.24.2.
2. *On Benefits* 2.22.1.
3. *On Benefits* 2.23.1.

This is what we ourselves were after when we decided, as a congregation, that the third mandate of our mission statement should be "GO to serve Christ." Knowing Christ and the immeasurable benefits Christ brings into our lives must lead to grateful response in the form of witness and service. Growing more like Christ must translate into putting ourselves—our time, our energies, our resources, our very bodies and all that can be accomplished through them—at God's disposal, even as Jesus had done, to advance God's interests in and to serve God's desires for the people and the world around us. Indeed, the level of our investment in witnessing and giving back to God through serving his interests reflects the level at which we value—or, frankly, do *not* value—the gifts we have received or are yet to receive.

* * *

The author of Hebrews clearly understands gratitude to involve us in *service*—again, in his words: "Let us not forget to do good and to share, for such sacrifices are well-pleasing to God" (Heb 13:16). In our mission statement, we emphasize "going" to serve Christ, which is good—we have to get out of this building and into the world. But the author of Hebrews points us to one another in the body of Christ as our first arena of service.

> Keep loving one another as sisters and brothers love each other. Don't neglect showing hospitality, for in this way some have entertained angels without knowing it. Remember those in chains as though chained yourselves alongside them, those who are being mistreated as though you yourselves are in their skin. (Heb 13:1–3)

The needs within our own congregation are significant and the needs of our harassed and persecuted sisters and brothers abroad, staggering. The care and compassion we show one another, the time and energy and resources we invest in relieving one another, here in this congregation as well as throughout the global body of Christ, are investments in people about whom God deeply cares, service that God receives as rendered even to himself. These are the spiritual and bloodless sacrifices that ascend before God and proclaim loudly and genuinely in his hearing, "Thank you, God, for all that you have brought into our lives."

* * *

The author of Hebrews, however, also impels us to give expression to our gratitude in the form of testimony and witness: "Through Jesus Christ, let us always offer to God the 'sacrifice of praise'—the fruit of lips that profess his name" (Heb 13:15). It is obvious when we offer "the sacrifice of praise" in this place, singing our hymns to God and offering prayers of thanksgiving. The author of Hebrews points to the less obvious but even more necessary "sacrifice of praise" when we own God *out there* with our lips, when we acknowledge, or confess, or *profess* God out there, testifying to the good things God has done for us, the help God has brought us, God's saving interventions in our lives and in the lives of those whom we love. Every such "sacrifice of praise," every such act of witness that we make to God's kindness, goodness, and beneficent intervention, is an invitation to our conversation partner to experience the same—and, as such, is an act of service of the greatest value to our neighbor.

D. T. Niles, a Sri Lankan pastor and evangelist of the twentieth century, eventually president of the Methodist Church of Ceylon, once said that evangelism "is just one beggar telling another beggar where to find bread." This is a profound and justly celebrated quotation, for it tells us how we need to see ourselves and others, how we need to see ourselves in regard to the other—*both* beggars, *one* of whom has found a place that never fails to give out bread. It also tells us how we need to value Christ, what he brought and continues to bring into our lives, and what he has for the other person—the life-sustaining nourishment of which our neighbor stands in as much need as we did and do.

I remember what it was like going back to school, as a kid, after Christmas break. I was excited to tell my friends about the great toys that I had received, and they were all excited to tell us about the great toys they had received. We would end up going to each other's houses and playing together with all these great, new toys. Witness—evangelism—is a lot like that. Only the better analogy is not boys and their toys, but beggars and bread, finding that which will nourish us, sustain us, get us through. Of course, even that analogy suffers, for witness— evangelism—is about sharing where to find life-giving bread of an entirely different and greater order. In Jesus' own words on the subject: "I am the living bread that came down from heaven. Whoever eats of *this* bread will live forever" (John 6:51 NRSV).

If we are ever to love our neighbors as we love ourselves, how can we keep back from them the invitation to enjoy what has been the most beneficial relationship that we have found, the connection with God through Christ that gains for us the greatest help for this life and the greatest hope for what follows this life? Whose good are we serving if we exert ourselves to give them a loaf of bread but falter at taking the extra step—the *eternally significant* extra step—of offering them the life-giving Bread that came down from heaven?

* * *

Perhaps we shy away from witness—from evangelism—because we think of it as walking someone down a theological argument like the "Romans Road" or as imposing our religion on someone else. That's all wrong. Witness—evangelism—is nothing more and nothing less than telling another person how God reached into our lives and turned things around for the better, turned us in a better direction. It is simply telling another person about the life-giving nourishment that we found and that is available for him or her as well.

As you come to know Christ and Christ's benefits more fully, allow yourself to be moved to witness and service in grateful response, simply sharing what you yourself have come to know of Christ and of his interventions in your life. As you keep growing more like Christ and seeing what God's transforming power and purpose can accomplish in your own life and in the lives of your sisters and brothers, simply bear witness to what you have experienced. In so doing, you are fulfilling that climactic commission that Christ entrusted to all of his followers when he said: "Go, then; make disciples out of all the nations" (Matt 28:18-20). Honor Christ's lordship and make his reign visible and real in this world, because it is visible and real in you, in your life, in our life together, as we give ourselves over to Christ, for him to accomplish his good purposes in this world through us, both offering his love and issuing his invitation through us. Go, indeed, to serve Christ. Amen.

Appendix

Correspondences with the Revised Common Lectionary

John 14:15–21 (Sermon 17)

Year A: Sixth Sunday of Easter

John 15:26–27; 16:4b–15 (Sermon 13)

Year B: Day of Pentecost

John 17:1–11 (Sermon 27)

Year A: Seventh Sunday of Easter

Acts 1:1–11 (Sermon 12)

Year A, B, C: Ascension of the Lord

Acts 2:1–21 (Sermon 16)

Year A, B, C: Day of Pentecost

Romans 6:1b–11 (Sermon 5)

Year A: Season after Pentecost—Proper 7 (12)

Romans 6:3–11 (Sermon 5)

Year A, B, C: Easter Vigil

Romans 8:1–11 (Sermon 14)

Year A: Season after Pentecost—Proper 10 (15)

Romans 8:6–11 (Sermon 14)

Year A: Fifth Sunday in Lent

Romans 8:12–17 (Sermon 14)

Year B: Trinity Sunday

Romans 8:26–39 (Sermon 28)

Year A: Season after Pentecost—Proper 12 (17)

1 Corinthians 12:1–11 (Sermon 15)

Year C: Second Sunday after the Epiphany

1 Corinthians 12:3b–13 (Sermon 15)

Year A: Day of Pentecost

1 Corinthians 15:19–26 (Sermon 11)

Year C: Easter Day (Resurrection of the Lord)

1 Corinthians 15:51–58 (Sermon 11)

Year C: Eighth Sunday after the Epiphany

Year C: Season after Pentecost—Proper 3 (8)

Hebrews 11:29–12:2 (Sermon 19)

Year C: Season after Pentecost—Proper 15 (20)

Hebrews 12:1–3 (Sermon 19)

Year A, B, C: Wednesday of Holy Week

Hebrews 12:18–29 (Sermon 29)

Year C: Season after Pentecost—Proper 16 (21)

Hebrews 13:1–8, 15–16 (Sermon 29)

Year C: Season after Pentecost—Proper 17 (22)

2 Peter 1:16–21 (Sermon 6)

Year A: Transfiguration Sunday

1 John 1:1–2:2 (Sermon 8)

Year B: Second Sunday of Easter

Revelation 7:9–17 (Sermon 25)

Year C: Fourth Sunday of Easter

Year A: All Saints Day

Scripture Index

Passages that are the primary texts for sermons are in bold.